True Love Dates is a wonderful dating/love/relationship resource for young women. I absolutely love that it instills our self-worth and value as daughters of God and teaches us to look for his best in our potential mate while refining ourselves as true ladies, leaders, and lovers in Christ. This is an absolute must-read and pivotal for any woman no matter your age or relationship history.

—Kristen Dalton, Miss America 2009,
Founder of ShelsMore.com

Hands down, the best book on dating that I've ever read! If you're single, this is a must-read. Jam-packed with wise counsel, Debra becomes your personal mentor as she answers dozens of real-life dating and relationship questions. Pastors and church leaders, get this resource into the hands of your singles!

—Chris Reed, Pastor to 20s/30s and Singles, Saddleback Church,
Lake Forest, CA

What a refreshing perspective on a critical topic. Deb's experiences and encounters are so direct and applicable to relationships not only with the opposite sex but also with Christ. So many relationships end badly because people put God in a box outside of their relationships, but Deb encourages us and directs us to how God wants to be right at the center of it all.

—ANDY KING, executive director,
Dream Center Peoria

TRUE LOVE
DATES

DEBRA K. FILETA, MA, LPC

TRUE LOVE DATES

DATES

YOUR INDISPENSABLE GUIDE *to* FINDING

THE LOVE OF YOUR LIFE

ZONDERVAN

True Love Dates
Copyright © 2013 by Debra K. Fileta

This title is also available as a Zondervan ebook. Visit www.zondervan.com/ebooks.

Requests for information should be addressed to:

Zondervan, 3900 *Sparks Dr. SE, Grand Rapids, Michigan* 49546

Library of Congress Cataloging-in-Publication Data

Fileta, Debra K.
    True love dates : your indispensable guide to finding the love of your life / Debra K.
Fileta, M.A., LPC. - 1st [edition].
       pages cm
    Includes bibliographical references.
    ISBN 978-0-310-33679-2 (softcover)
    1. Man-woman relationships - Religious aspects - Christianity. 2. Dating (Social
customs) - Religious aspects - Christianity. 3. Mate selection - Religious aspects-
Christianity. I. Title.
BT705.8.F55 2013
241'.6765 - dc23
                2013018186

Published in association with literary agent Blair Jacobson of D.C. Jacobson & Associates LLC, an Author Management Company, www.dcjacobson.com

The names and identifying information of people discussed in this book have been changed to protect their identities and to respect their confidentiality.

Cover photography: *Rayes/Getty Images®*
Interior design: *Sarah Johnson*

First printing September 2013 / Printed in the United States of America

To my love, John:
You have added so richly to my understanding
of true love because of the way you've loved me.
I will love you forever.

. . .

To my beautiful babies, Ella and Elijah:
My prayer is that you may come to know God's true
love for you in a powerful way and that this love will
overflow onto everyone around you.

CONTENTS

ACKNOWLEDGMENTS

Before all else, I want to give thanks to my first love, Jesus. You are the only reason this book exists. This has been your message from the moment it came into my mind, and I stand in awe that you chose to use me to share your words of hope with a generation that is hungry for True Love.

I want to say thank you to my husband, John. You have been my greatest support and encouragement from the moment I started writing. You believed in this book long before I even believed in it myself. Your love was the greatest inspiration as I wrote these words, and every page is a declaration of our forever true and undying love. "Go with me, my love."

Thank you to my mom and dad for shaping me into the woman I am today. Your love for God and constant sacrifice are behind so much of who I am and what I've become. Thank you for your love.

A huge thanks to my literary management team — Don and Blair Jacobson and the entire team at D. C. Jacobson and Associates: You saw something important in this message and helped me bring it to fruition. Thank you for your dedication to sharing God's love through the written word.

To my incredible team at Zondervan. Thank you for your commitment to this book. The publishing process has been an incredible journey of refinement in so many ways. God has used you to help make this book the best it can be. Thank you for believing in this message. An extra special thanks to Carolyn McCready for her constant support, feedback, and encouragement.

To everyone who has poured into my life or influenced my career — specifically Dr. Steven Hamon and the Antioch Group family; Professor Sundi Donovan; Pastor John King; instructors and teachers, pastors and mentors, friends and family. Your investment in my life has allowed me to invest in the lives of others. Thank you.

To God be the glory.

INTRODUCTION
Dating Inward, Outward, and Upward

"I do."

These are the words many single young adults dream of saying. I remember longing for the day when I could look into the eyes of the love of my life and utter those perfect two words in front of a crowd of witnesses. It would be such a sacred moment, filled with deep emotion and uncontainable joy.

But my "I do" moment wasn't quite what I expected it to be.

The night before our wedding, gorgeous linens were perfectly draped at the backdrop of the church. Flower arrangements lined each aisle. The wedding dress was pressed, the rings were safely secured, and the wedding party arrived in time from all over the country. With friends and family in town, we quickly finished our rehearsal, which went off without a hitch. I didn't really think too much about the details of the ceremony, because to be honest, I had seen more than a dozen weddings in the past few years and pretty much knew the drill. Soon after the rehearsal, we were off to have a good time and celebrate at our rehearsal dinner.

When our wedding day finally arrived, everything happened so quickly that it seemed as though the day was on fast-forward. Before I knew it, I was walking down the aisle toward my sweet teary-eyed husband-to-be and then, moments later, getting ready to finally say "I do."

As I listened to the pastor recite the beautiful words with which he asked me if I would "take this man to be my beloved husband," I realized something.

I had no idea which hand to place the ring on. His right or my left? Is that the same thing? There I was, in front of a crowd of more than three hundred people, with no idea what to do next.

So I grabbed a hand, and hoping no one would notice, I placed the ring on my beloved husband's ring finger.

But leave it to my loud and rambunctious family to tell it like it is. Sure enough, someone called me out.

"Wrong hand!" came a shout from the crowd, piercing the sacred moment and producing a ripple of chuckles throughout the chapel.

Trying to save the moment, I looked around and shouted back, "Wrong hand ... but at least I've got the right guy!"

After the laughter subsided, we regained our composure, got the ring on the right (left) hand, and went on with our vows.

Isn't that the truth when it comes to finding true love? So many things can be right on your wedding day: the perfect decor, the most elegant reception hall, the greatest group of family and friends, the right hand, and even the perfect "I do" moment, but without the right spouse, you've got nothing with which to move forward.

If you've picked up this book, it's likely that you're searching for true love. Your desire for marriage may be strong, even feel like a preoccupation that you can't seem to shake. You might be sick and tired of being single and alone, watching your friends get knocked off, one by one, into the world of love while you feel more and more isolated. Maybe you found someone you thought was "the one," only to have your heart broken and your hopes shattered, alone once again. In a world that seems to cater to couples and families, sitting at a table for one is the last place you want to be.

But the ironic thing about finding true love is that it must start at a table for one. The phrase "true love dates" means that before any significant relationship comes along, you must commit to a series of three stages of dating: inward, outward, and upward. Believe it or not, these stages begin with one very important person you may have overlooked: yourself.

In a world that idolizes relationships, the importance of getting to know yourself has been lost. Not only is it a significant step toward finding happiness, it is also a vital stop along the journey of finding true love. Dating inward is the first stage, the foundation on which every other stage builds.

Of course, finding true love doesn't stop there; this is only the beginning. True love dates because once you have dated yourself, the next step is dating others. In the course of dating outward, most relationships will be temporary, used only as tools to chisel and polish you. Dating outward should be seen as a learning process in the search for true love. It involves transparency, timing, communication, and healthy boundaries. It is a give-and-take that must never desperately give too much or fearfully give too little. It is a series of choices that lead you closer and closer to true love.

Once you have mastered the art of dating inward and learned from the complexities of dating outward, you're ready for the last step. Last, but oh so important, is dating upward. Dating upward is the practice of connecting to God, allowing your relationship with him to guide and shape your life.

Many skip over this step in their pursuit of true love, relying on their own definitions and examples of love to guide them. Dating upward proposes that to fully engage in the exchange of love with another human being, you must first experience it within the context of a relationship with God. Dating upward requires committing to your relationship with the designer and creator of true love. It involves accepting that you are loved by him, and then learning to reciprocate this love to God and to extend it to others. It means inviting God into the deepest parts of your heart, allowing his definition of love to permeate your life and, in turn, your relationships.

True love dates because it is within these three stages of dating that you can find true love — true love for yourself, true love for your future mate, and true love for God.

A note to the reader: throughout this book, you will find FAQ boxes with frequently asked questions in them. These FAQs are answered in chapter 13. As you read, feel free to flip to that chapter to find answers to the questions that most interest you.

PART ONE

DATING INWARD

CHAPTER 1

THE PERSON YOU NEVER THOUGHT YOU'D DATE

"Am I going to be single forever?"

She sat across from me on a comfortable, oversized gray chair. She was dressed in a professional pencil skirt, ruffled blouse, bright red shoes, and spunky narrow glasses that matched her spunky personality. Her tearstained cheeks reflected the sadness and confusion that she felt about this subject that had become such an important part of her heart.

Carrie had come to counseling for one reason and one reason alone — to sort through the pain of her singleness. She was in her late twenties, and she thought for sure she would be married by now. But God's timeline didn't seem to match up with hers. She was struggling with being alone and single

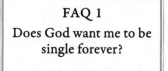

FAQ 1

Does God want me to be single forever?

while all her friends were happily married. She'd had enough of being the third wheel. When would it be her turn to find true love?

I know for certain that Carrie is not the only one who is thinking and feeling this way about love. I remember a class I took my freshman year of college that proved this to be true. The professor asked us to consider the plans we had for our future and to put together a three-minute presentation on our ambitions and dreams.

The results were pretty typical. Some hoped to be doctors, a few lawyers, and others teachers.

But there was one presentation that was so unexpected that I will likely never forget it. One young woman sweetly waltzed up to the podium and began to share her dreams and ambitions. In her southern belle accent, she boldly proclaimed her desire to be a wife and a mother as the passion of her life. Without a hint of shame, she explained that she was at college with one thing in mind: to get her "MRS degree." To enter college as a Ms. and leave as a Mrs. was her top priority in life.

I can't say that this way of thinking was foreign to me, because I too had the strong desire to find a spouse and get married someday. But the fact that she actually said it out loud confirmed the reality that so many people are looking for love.

In the past few years of my practice as a professional counselor, I have seen numerous young men and women just like Carrie, men and women who are struggling to come to terms with the truth that the future they had envisioned for themselves looks starkly different from the reality that they are living, men and women who are hoping and praying that they will one day get to say those two simple words, "I do."

THE SIGNIFICANCE OF "I DO"

It is a phrase that has profound impact on the lives of those who speak it. Two little words that hold so much power, fusing two separate lives and two separate hearts into one. Though countless men and women have uttered "I do," I wonder how many of them have considered the depth of this phrase. It's a phrase that begins with personal responsibility and insight, because in order to proclaim "I do," one has to know and understand "I."

For thousands of years, the greatest thinkers of all time have come to the same conclusion that living a meaningful life comes down to this one thing. Aristotle said that "knowing yourself is the beginning of all wisdom." Pascal reinforced this way of thinking in his plea to mankind that "one must know oneself." So how did our philosophy on finding love get so fixated on looking out rather than looking in?

In Psalm 139, the psalmist marvels at God's complete knowledge of us. The fact that a God who is so powerful has such a detailed knowledge of and interest in our lives is simply mind boggling. He is keenly aware of us, from the moment we wake to the moment we close our eyes. And after verse upon verse of reveling in God's knowledge of us comes a tiny phrase that turns the focus back to "I": "Your works are wonderful, I know that full well" (Ps. 139:14).

Did you get that? Read it again. After going on about how we are God's workmanship, the psalmist proclaims, "Your works are wonderful, I know that full well." In other words, the psalm could go like this: "God, you made me in a marvelous way. I am your masterpiece, and I know that whatever you make is wonderful."

Is that true in your life? Do you know full well that you are God's workmanship? Do you really believe that you are wonderful, simply because you are God's? Do you grasp the details that make you who you are? Do you have an awareness of yourself in the same way that your Creator has an awareness of you?

DATING INWARD

We live in a society that is so fixated on knowing others. Young men and women are encouraged to get out there and date, to get to know people in the hope of finding a permanent match. They spend months — even years — in pursuit of the person they hope to spend the rest of their lives with, forgetting that the rest of their lives in marriage involves not just one individual but two.

At the end of the season of dating, you will have invested copious amounts of energy and countless hours getting to know the person you will be standing with at the altar, but what about the other person?

What about yourself?

God understands the importance of looking inward. The Bible teaches us to "love your neighbor as yourself" (Matt. 22:39). Loving others is contingent on the ability to love yourself. The ironic thing is that many singles are ready to get out there and love someone else, but they haven't taken the time to love themselves. Loving yourself requires that you know, value, and respect the person you are while moving toward the person God has made you to be. But somehow this important truth gets moved to the back burner. We tend to focus so much on the first part of this verse that calls us to love others that we neglect to love ourselves.

I have to admit that for a while I was missing this piece of the puzzle. I spent so much of my young adult years looking for true love without ever getting to know and appreciate who I was. I read book after book on dating and courtship in an attempt to learn all that I could about meeting, identifying, and interacting with my soul mate. I focused on building a relationship not realizing how much of *me* that relationship would one day entail. I put a lot of effort into finding "the one," all the while losing myself.

I grew up in a generation that was stuck between two very different ways of thinking about how to find true love. Inside the church, I was bombarded with messages regarding courtship and commitment. Gender roles were clear. Men were to be the pursuers, and women were to be the pursued. Chivalry was a must, and whether a man opened the door for a woman was almost as important as the condition of his soul. Dating was seen as the pagan way of living. One had to kiss dating goodbye and pursue true love through courtship: long-term, deeply committed, smooch-free relationships that were headed toward marriage. This mentality left absolutely no room for dating, because if you were planning on having coffee with someone, you had better know that they were "the one." Talk about some serious pressure.

The other way of thinking about how to find true love pervaded the world outside the church, and I encountered it in the movies I watched and in the magazines I read and in the lives of people I interacted with. Chivalry was seen as a weakness and gender roles were considered confining. Dating around was the only way to find true love, and moving in together was the only way to test it. Commitment was an old-fashioned word, laden with fear and anxiety. Afraid to make the wrong choice in a partner, my generation decided to refrain from choosing altogether. Why risk it all on one when you could have as many as you wanted "risk-free"?

As a Christian young adult, I found myself struggling to make sense of two starkly different ways of thinking, neither of which seemed to accurately define me or offer me a practical way to live. I took on the stories of others as my own, trying to relive their experiences and recreate their romance in the hope that these things would lead me to love. Instead, I was led down a road of confusion and pain.

I came from a fairly conservative family that didn't encourage dating in my teens. I spent a lot of my time with friends and was involved in church activities. But as much as I enjoyed my high school years, I longed for the day when I could be in an exclusive dating relationship. Upon entering college, I

> **FAQ 2**
> What are some practical ways to date inward?

was finally free to make my own decisions when it came to dating. And lucky for me, there were single, good-looking young men everywhere I looked.

Impatient to be in a relationship, I found myself dating the very first guy who showed an interest in me. He was a sweet young man, gracious and kind in every way. But in my craving for attention and connection, I failed to recognize that he was not right for me. Because I had no awareness of who I was or what I needed, I found myself settling for a mediocre relationship rather than holding out for what was best.

Trying to stay true to the concept of courtship that I had read about and so desperately wanted to believe in, I confined myself to a relationship that I eventually knew in my heart wasn't the right fit. I was terrified of failure and of letting people down. Afraid of starting over, afraid of playing the dating game, I allowed my bond to get deeper and deeper with a man whom I ultimately would not marry.

After two years of heartache, I finally let go of this relationship and for the first time in my life engaged in dating inward. My relationship with God was strengthened, as was my awareness of myself and, in turn, my relationships with others. The more awareness I gained, the more I grew in confidence and was empowered to trust my heart again. Rather than allowing the stories of others to define my love life, I found the God-given wisdom to create my own story.

THE PERSON YOU NEVER THOUGHT YOU'D DATE

Dating inward may be the most important component of your story because it is not dependent on anyone else. You don't even have to be in a relationship to get started. When you're single, it's easier to focus on what you don't have than on what you do. It's difficult to change that focus in a culture that defines the word *single* as "incomplete." Dating inward requires a change of perspective, a shift in thinking that puts the focus on who you are rather than whom you are with. And the only commitment it requires is a commitment to yourself.

Getting to know yourself may seem simple, and on the one hand it is. It is as simple as strolling into an art gallery, yet as complex as closely observing, analyzing, and finding meaning in each and every piece of art. The difficulty comes in choosing how much you will allow yourself to engage and discover, how much you will allow yourself to come face to face with the person you never thought you would date: yourself.

Many people have little to no awareness of who they are. Others see their true self as a part of them that they have to hide from pain, brokenness, abandonment, abuse, and fear. It's the part that may be covered with insecurities or painted with pride. Either way, it's part of them. And it needs to be exposed *to them* for healthy relationships to become a possibility.

Author Julien Green says that "the greatest explorer on this earth never takes voyages as long as those of the man who descends to the depth of his heart." When you choose to look inward, you are choosing to go where no man has gone before, because only you have access to this terrain. It is a journey that brings with it new discoveries each and every day.

WHERE DO I BEGIN?

Maybe you're realizing how much time you've spent pursuing others and how very little time you've spent pursuing yourself. Maybe you acknowledge that in trying to find someone to love, you have actually lost yourself. Maybe these concepts resonate within your heart and you are ready to embark on this experience. So what does it mean to date inward? How do you get to know yourself?

When it comes to self-discovery, I find it helpful to begin by answering three questions:

1. Where do I come from?
2. Where and who am I now?
3. Where am I going?

Each question is an important component in getting to know yourself and requires you to take the time to learn, explore, and discover. Each answer offers fresh perspectives and insights, and challenges you to see yourself in a whole new way. The next three chapters of this book will guide you in answering each question as you begin this voyage of self-discovery.

If you are ever to relate fully to another person, you must begin by dating yourself. Foundational to knowing what you need in a partner is knowing who you are. Are you ready to get to know the person you never thought you'd date?

Questions for Reflection

1. What are some ways our culture emphasizes dating others as the key to finding true love?

2. In your journey of finding true love, how much time and energy have you devoted to getting to know yourself?

3. What do you believe about yourself? Do you see yourself as God's workmanship? Do you know full well that his works (including you) are wonderful? If not, what is holding you back?

CHAPTER 2

WHERE DO I COME FROM?
The Colors of Our Past

"The way you do the things you do." — the Temptations

There's a funny story about a new bride who always cut off the end of her ham when she prepared it for dinner. When her husband asked why, she replied, "I don't know. My mom always did it that way, so I just thought that's how it is supposed to be done." Out of curiosity, the bride called her mother and asked the reason for cutting off the end of the ham. The mother replied, "I'm not really sure. That's just the way your grandma always did it when I was growing up." A little while later, when the bride was visiting her grandmother, she asked, "Grandma, why do you always cut off the end of the ham when you bake it?" The grandmother replied, "Well, I had to, dear; otherwise it would never fit in my small pan."

As lighthearted and humorous as this story sounds, the reality is that we are shaped by what we have learned from those around us. So much of my time in both premarital and marital counseling sessions is spent tracing the steps that led a couple to their problems and pain. I spend hour after hour digging into their pasts to identify solutions for their present, because knowing your past is crucial to succeeding in your present.

OUR FIRST CONFLICT

It was the week of Christmas. The stockings were hung, the tree was decorated, the scent of delicious food was flowing through the house, and snowflakes were falling gently to the ground on a beautiful, chilly Chicago day. It was the perfect postcard picture of family fun and relaxation. John and I were visiting his family, celebrating our first Christmas together as a married couple. And while everyone was downstairs playing board games and munching on delicious snacks, John came upstairs to find me in tears.

As much as I tried to have fun and enjoy my time with my new family, it was nothing like what I was used to. My family spent Christmas week shopping, traveling, and visiting family and friends together. There was so much to see and do, and we found joy in the hustle and bustle of the Christmas season. On the other hand, John's family celebrated the entire week in the comfort of their cozy home. They valued spending quality time with one another, away from distractions and the busyness of the outside world — no shopping, no traveling, no hustle and bustle. As much as I loved his family, I didn't think I could take one more moment of quality time and being indoors. With tears streaming down my face, I explained to him that I missed my family and our way of celebrating Christmas. For the first time in our marriage, differences stemming from our family origins had birthed a conflict.

FAMILY OF ORIGIN

Our family of origin plays a lead role in determining who we are. It makes sense when you think about it. Nearly everything we know and feel about ourselves has roots in the soil of our upbringing. We learn about communication from watching our parents. Our self-esteem and value are based on words and actions that were imprinted on our minds from a young age. Our desire for love and acceptance is either satisfied or parched by our family atmosphere.

Even our views of sex and sexuality stem from our exposure to our families' attitudes about them in our early years.

A lucky few have fond memories of a home filled with love, affection, fidelity, and honesty. Their families solved problems with proper communication, expressed feelings in a healthy way, and exchanged love and support freely. But most people experienced the good, the bad, and the ugly in their families. Maybe you come from a home where communication had two forms: silence or rage. Maybe love was felt but never articulated. Maybe you grew up longing for acceptance, but acceptance was never given. Maybe you live with the wounds of divorce, fatherlessness, religious hypocrisy, physical or sexual abuse, alcoholism, or addiction.

> **FAQ 3**
> My parents are divorced and have always had a rocky marriage. I've heard divorce runs in families. Am I destined to go down this road as well?

Whatever your past was like, stepping back and looking at the big picture is the first step in answering the question, Where do I come from? It involves addressing the hurts that have caused pain and anger, identifying the dysfunction that has produced fear and doubt, and considering the broken relationships that have led to anxiety and mistrust. Understanding where you come from means taking a good hard look at your past and giving yourself the freedom to learn from it.

Understanding can lead to liberation. Knowledge can bring freedom from the past. For those who don't take the time to understand their past and are blind to how it has shaped them, the road to true love can be difficult.

CATHERINE'S STORY

Catherine was born in a country town in southern Alabama. She grew up with her mom and dad and four brothers and was surrounded by roughhousing and pranks. She was a sweet girl, a southern belle with the kindest heart and purest smile. But Catherine was stuck in a pattern of relationships that was anything but sweet and pure.

She entered my office just days after being beaten by her partner. I used the word *abuse*, while she used the words *relationship problem*. Unfortunately, this was not new for Catherine. She had been in numerous physically and verbally abusive relationships.

Catherine did some soul-searching in our therapy sessions. We took a good, hard look at the picture her past had painted for her. And sure enough, there was a clear link between the colors of her past and the colors of her present.

Growing up with an alcoholic father, Catherine was used to the emotional instability that came with the highs and lows of addictions. To her, this was normal. Never really feeling love and acceptance from her emotionally absent father, she longed for a relationship that would fill her up inside. Ironically, she found herself drawn to men who were just like her father. She thought that if she worked hard enough and loved strong enough, this time around, she could get the man in her life to change. She could get him to love her.

> **FAQ 4**
> How do I know whether I am in a toxic relationship?

When Jeremy came along, he seemed to do the trick. With words of "love" spewing out of his mouth, he filled a void she was desperate to fill — so much so that she made exceptions for his anger. After all, in her mind that seemed to be the norm in families. And the verbal abuse? "Well, I'm sure I could get him to fix that once we're really committed." And the physical violence? "Well, it's only when he gets really angry. And his anger is usually my fault anyway. I just need to learn to stay away from his buttons and be more loving."

The colors of her past — experiences from her family of origin that she was accustomed to, that felt familiar, that seemed normal, experiences that God had never intended her to have — were bleeding into her present.

Maybe you can relate to Catherine's story. Maybe there is something about the void she felt that resonates with your life, reminding you of a past filled with parental absence, lack of affection, and mixed messages. Or maybe you connect with her "rescuer" mentality, with the hope that you can fill that empty part of you by fixing the broken world around you with your love.

Or maybe you can't relate. Maybe you see her story as out of the ordinary.

But even though your past may not have been as volatile and dysfunctional as hers, the truth is that the colors of your past still find their way into the picture of your present.

JULIA'S STORY

Compared with Catherine, Julia had a rather good life. She grew up in a Christian home surrounded by support, faith, and family values. It seemed as though a healthy future was inevitable, except for one thing: Julia's mother.

Julia's mother seemed to be a confident woman — sometimes a little too confident. For Julia's mother, "no" was not a viable answer. It was her way or the highway. Julia remembers growing up with a sense of respect for her mother, coupled with great fear. As long as she behaved "like a good girl," things were fine. But the moment her choices or wishes got in the way of her mother's desires, there was turmoil. Conflict, anger, and resentment set in and their relationship was severed. Julia grew up unable to recognize her own desires and dreams; she learned to stifle them without even realizing it. Having been controlled by another, Julia grew up without a true sense of self: no freedom to grow, to make mistakes, or to develop independence.

I met Julia when she and her husband came in for therapy with a problem that was ironic, considering Julia's indecisive background: Julia's anger was seeping into her marriage. She found herself getting angry at her husband for the slightest things: the way he folded his clothes, the way he chewed his gum, the way he was so laid back. Every little thing seemed to grate on her until she exploded. Julia had become a control freak. Having lived in an atmosphere in which her personal control had been taken away, she was overcompensating to gain it back. Without realizing it, Julia was exhibiting the characteristics she hated so much in her mother. The colors of her past had bled into the picture of her present.

GOOD INTENTIONS, BAD MEMORIES

I recently received an email from a young man who was wrestling with the negative impact that his past was having on him, particularly in the area of love and relationships. He explained that he had come from a good Christian home with godly parents who truly loved the Lord. They were great parents who invested their time, affection, and love in his life. The problem was that they didn't always seem to love each other.

He remembers growing up with constant bickering and fighting as part of the family atmosphere. He hated how his parents acted when they were upset, but even more, he hated the apathy he saw in their relationship. Now that he was in his twenties, his parents' negative view of each other and their mediocre relationship were taking their toll on him, causing him to wonder if this is all that Christian marriage and romantic relationships would ever crack up to be. Even though he grew up in a well-meaning and loving family, he found himself battling memories of his past.

You, too, may come from a well-meaning family who did their best to love and raise you. Even so, it's important to recognize that there is no such thing as a perfect family. All parents, no matter how well-intentioned they may be, pass down both helpful and harmful habits to their children. It's important for you to come to terms with this fact and acknowledge your parents for who they actually are: valuable human beings made in the image of God but flawed and burdened by the effects of sin, negative experiences, and even their own families of origin.

Understanding these things is important, but even in your awareness, you may still be asking, like the young man in the email, How do I overcome the demons of my past?

WHAT TO DO WITH OUR PAST

One of the greatest factors that inhibits people from moving forward is their past. The Bible describes a woman who also wrestled with the demons of her past. God had called Lot and his wife out of Sodom and into something new. He'd called them out of the darkness of their past and into a new beginning, out of the sin and struggles that surrounded them and into something better, something greater. But Lot's wife was unable to let go of the past, of what was behind her. In fact, Scripture explains that she looked back and "became a pillar of salt" (Gen. 19:26).

The past can be paralyzing. The past numbs many people, preventing them from experiencing their present and moving into their future. Maybe you can relate. Maybe the past has wrapped its tentacles around your heart. God is calling you to look ahead (Phil. 3:13). Here are some ways to break free:

1. *Accept your past.* No matter how dark or difficult your past may be, it is crucial that you come to terms with the reality that it cannot be changed; it may never be forgotten, but it can always be used. God can take the wounds of your past

and use them to strengthen, sharpen, and shape you into who he wants you to be today.

For some, accepting the past comes with the healing power of time, God's relentless grace, and a whole lot of support. But for others, the process is much more complicated. If you find that you are unable to live in the present because of the burdens of your past, be open to seeking the help of a professional. Find a Christian counselor in your area and give yourself the chance to confront, process, and accept your past.

> ### FAQ 5
> How do I know whether I need professional counseling to help me work through my past?

2. *Understand your present.* More significant than what has happened in your past is who you have become in the present. Though the past may shape your present, it can't control it. By the grace of God, you are enabled to overcome your past by becoming who God has called you to be here and now. No matter what lies behind you, God has placed you where you are at today "for such a time as this" (Est. 4:14). Find your purpose, identify your passions, and live for the present.

3. *Envision your future.* Having a vision for your life is of ultimate importance. Scripture explains that "where there is no vision, the people perish" (Prov. 29:18 KJV). The ability to live in the present grounds you, but living with hope for the future propels you forward. What do you imagine your life will look like in one year, five years, or ten years? Where do you hope to be? What do you hope to be doing? Open your heart, release your mind, trust your spirit, and begin envisioning your future.

No matter how dark your past may be, God is ready to shine his light in the darkest of places. He can bring health and wholeness to places that you thought never could be healed. It's time to trust God with your history and allow him to help you fix your eyes on his story for your life. And remember, the result is not perfection; it's healthy perspective.

PERSPECTIVE VERSUS PERFECTION

Even if it were possible to identify all of the ways our past has shaped us, there would be no way to resolve every flaw we find. Human beings are works in progress. Every day is another step toward discovering the best version of ourselves.

Dating inward has nothing to do with perfection and everything to do with perspective. It is the process of learning to see yourself as you really are rather than as you want to be. That's a difficult thing to do.

I attended a church meeting where the pastor asked the members of the congregation to raise their hands if they thought that the church was a serving church. About ninety percent of the group raised their hands. Then the pastor asked for a show of hands from those who gave up more than one hour of their time every week to serve those in need. This time, only a few hands made their way into the air. The pastor noted, "By the showing of hands, there is clearly a huge difference between who you think you are and who you really are."

How many of us are guilty of that same thing — living under the disguise of who we want to be rather than coming to terms with who we actually are? We look for the perfect mate not realizing that we have neglected the perfecting of ourselves. Finding true love starts with taking inventory of our strengths and weaknesses, quirks and traits, hopes and dreams, and getting to know the person behind the mask.

The beautiful thing about healthy perspective is that it is only the beginning. When we understand how our past has shaped us, we cannot remain the same. New knowledge demands a response.

It requires a movement toward change. It fuels action. In the wise words of Maya Angelou, "When you know better, you do better."

LISA'S STORY

For the first time in many years, Lisa had entered into a season of singleness. She had a history of dating the wrong guys, one after another. With the perspective allowed by her pause from dating, Lisa realized that the people she dated were nothing like the man she had always dreamed of marrying. She had a tendency to settle, living in the hope of what she wanted the relationship to become rather than seeing it for what it was.

When I met Lisa, she was ready to make some discoveries about herself. She was sick and tired of doing things the same old way and was ready for a transformation. And she was willing to do the work that this required.

After I took some time to understand Lisa's life and her past, it became clear to me that many of the patterns that were holding her back stemmed from things she learned in her family of origin. The dynamics of Lisa's relationship with her parents and of her parents' relationship with each other had set the stage for her future relationships in a way that she never could have imagined.

Lisa opened up about her mother, a Christian woman who was content with being miserable in her marriage. As Lisa was growing up, her mother had always complained to her about her marriage, but never made the necessary changes. Unknowingly, her mother conveyed the message that settling in relationships was inevitable, that a perfect relationship could never be found. Lisa had taken this message to heart. If God's best didn't really exist for her, she might as well settle for someone who was "good enough."

Lisa's relationship with her father had also played a role. She spoke with tears in her eyes about the distance she felt from him, never feeling loved or appreciated, respected or adored. He took care of her physical needs for food and shelter, but her emotional needs were left unmet. No affection, no praise, no connection. She was hungry for that kind of love, and shortly after she went off to college, she began to take it from anyone who offered it.

Looking back on her life and the factors that affected her decisions was a really important step in Lisa's healing process. She began to expose faulty ways of thinking that she had never questioned before. She processed this new information and allowed it to transform her life. She started making decisions based on the truth that God had shown her through his Word and through counseling.

Lisa is proof that when you know better, you do better. Her new understanding had a profound impact on her life; slowly she began looking at dating in a new light. She made up her mind not to settle for less than God's best, and she took the next few months to invest in herself by allowing God to heal her emotional wounds before she reentered the world of dating.

This, my friends, is the ultimate goal of dating yourself. It is the art of digging deep and taking a hard look at where you have come from in order to light the path to where you are going. It is the process of learning from your past as you are empowered to choose your future. It is the opportunity to get real with yourself in the most intimate and transparent way. It is the journey of taking the pain of your past and turning it into perspective as you make changes for a healthier future. It's time to look forward and be freed.

Questions for Reflection

1. How have the colors of your past bled into the picture of your present?
2. In your family of origin, how was love communicated? How were emotions expressed? How was conflict managed?

3. Have you committed to working through the pain of your past in order to gain perspective? If yes, how will you begin this process? If no, what is standing in your way?

4. Is there an area of your life in which you now "know better so you will do better"? How might this part of your life change with your renewed perspective?

CHAPTER 3

WHO AM I NOW?
A Picture Paints a Thousand Words

"Mirror, mirror, on the wall…"

My husband always comments on the fact that I can't seem to walk by a mirror without looking into it. He's pretty much right. Some people might think that's a little vain, but the reality is I don't know anyone who doesn't take a peek at their appearance when they get the chance.

The whole point of a mirror is this: growth and change. No one approaches a mirror unless they intend to come face to face with who they are, and one hundred percent of the time, something in that reflection requires change: a loose hair, a little green fleck on a tooth, the beginnings of a pimple. It seems that there is always something that needs fixing.

The amazing thing about a mirror is that it offers us nothing but a reflection. No comments, no advice, no suggestions. A simple reflection. It's up to us to change.

A thought-provoking passage in the book of James challenges us to get real with how we look. Not on the outside but on the inside. It talks about the importance of spiritual growth and explains that a person who listens to God's words but doesn't change is like a person who looks in the mirror but walks away, forgetting what they saw (James 1:23 – 25).

A tragedy occurs when you come face to face with yourself but leave unchanged. There is danger in closing your eyes to who you are, never stopping to reflect. But this is the most important component to dating yourself — reflecting on the face in the mirror and allowing yourself to ask, Who am I?

BIRDS OF A FEATHER

"Birds of a feather flock together." That saying is true in so many ways. The reality of dating is that you are attracted to people who are similar to you, similar not necessarily in appearance or personality (though that may be true) but in health.

I can't tell you the number of times I have counseled men and women who have asked me through tears, "Why am I always attracted to the unhealthy ones?" The simple answer is that what you believe about yourself is what you will get. Your beliefs and view of self are so central to determining the kind of person you will relate to. They act like lures, drawing people to your side. Your level of emotional health and self-esteem will always attract others who are in the same category. Healthy people will marry healthy people because you will always end up with the person whom you believe you deserve. It's a simple equation, though we tend to complicate it.

It's almost as though human beings are magnetic. We attract people who are similar to us. Not only that, but studies on dating[1] have shown that we even tend to date and marry people who are similar to us in appearance and style. If something as superficial as physical appearance holds that much power, how much more magnetic is the influence of our mental and emotional world?

IDENTITY CRISIS

The blinking red and blue lights in my rearview mirror definitely caught my attention. What can I say? I have an issue with speed limits. One of my cousins swears she's allergic to them, so maybe it's genetic.

As I rolled down my window, the officer looked inside and cut straight to the point. "Can I see some ID?" I scrambled to find my identification in the bottomless pit I call my purse, and handed it to him, smiling, hoping that my pearly whites would work their magic. (They didn't.)

It's amazing that one little card holds so much value when it comes to defining us. With just one swipe, the officer was able to take a small look into my life: name, height, weight, eye color, and good guy/bad guy status in the eyes of the law. It makes me wonder, if we were each in charge of writing our identification cards, what the description would be.

In other words, who do you think you are?

It's an important question, because without your being aware of it, your beliefs about yourself drive so much of what you choose in life. Your identity determines what and even whom you will identify with, because human beings are drawn to what is familiar.

I remember hearing of a social study that was conducted on large groups of strangers who were placed in a room together. The participants ranged widely in age, race, gender, and socioeconomic status. The researchers watched to see what the participants would do when given the opportunity to interact with one another. Time and time again throughout the study, people who were alike ended up together. Whether they were bonding because of their race, gender, or hair color, they found there was something attractive about people who were the same in some way. If identity has such an impact on mere strangers, how much more of an impact does it have when it comes to finding someone to love for life? How is it that such an important factor is so neglected?

STOLEN IDENTITIES

You've probably heard of the horrors that identity theft wreaks on the unsuspecting. Thieves use stolen identities to steal thousands of dollars, purchase extravagant items, and rack up major debt that threatens to destroy their victims.

It's sad to hear about these crimes and the innocent people they affect. But it's even more devastating to consider the theft that occurs each and every day in the lives of countless young men and women who have been robbed of their God-created identity.

Timothy was one of those young men. The rejection, discouragement, and insecurity that had been placed on him by his demanding father had robbed him of his identity, and he had taken upon himself an identity that he was never meant to possess. When he contacted me, he was struggling to separate his God-created self from the negative beliefs he had carried most of his life.

Young men and women all over the world are experiencing the same thing. An email from a young woman describes the challenge of pursuing a healthy identity: "I still struggle with what I think I deserve. Not surprisingly, when I went on a life-changing mission trip last year, I came to understand that I did not know my identity in Christ (never heard of it actually), and I believed all sorts of outrageous lies from the enemy. I hear 'find your identity in Christ' all the time now, but I want to know what that looks like for someone to work it out in their life."

The truth is that we are all in the midst of an identity struggle. Bombarded by cultural messages that fool us into believing that our identity is found in our appearance, prestige, and popularity, and lied to by our own internal dialogue, we are constantly engaged in conflict with an enemy of God who wants to rob us of who we we're made to be. God's Word describes Satan as a thief, coming only to "steal and kill and destroy" our lives and with them our perspective of who we're made to be (John 10:10). He is shameless, using whatever and whomever he can to beat us down and take away our hope. But no matter what obstacles Satan throws in our way, Jesus offers us life and the restoration of our identity: completeness and fullness in Christ (John 10:10).

But how does a person hear God's voice over the roar of all the other voices? What would God's voice even say? How do you distinguish who you are from who everyone else says you are? These are questions each and every person must struggle with. While I don't claim to have all the answers, I do know what worked for me. My beliefs about myself began to change as I rooted my identity in what God says.

RECLAIMING IDENTITY

Forming identity is a lifelong process of sorting through and applying information we receive about ourselves. Parents, family members, friends, teachers, significant others — the list of people who may have had a hand in shaping our identity is limitless. Add to this the effects of media, societal expectations, and cultural norms and it gets even more complicated. Our perspective of self can become skewed as we take in faulty information from the world around us, making it hard to uncover and apply God's truths.

I recently heard a talk about identity in which the speaker said that it's almost as though we are born into a world in which we are constantly being labeled by others — our parents, our friends, our family, and people we don't even know. Each person, from the outside looking in, comes up with a label to slap onto us without our permission. Some labels are kind and some are truthful, but many of them are lies. And sometimes we leave the negative labels on so long that we believe what they say; we allow those labels to define us.

God came to rip off all the false labels and to teach us the truth about who he made us to be. In my pursuit of healthy identity, God's truth was where I had to start, because it was the only opinion that I knew was unchanging. All the other things I had used to measure my value were inconsistent. Physical appearance, friendships, parental approval, grades, and accomplishments were all things that could either elate me or depress me depending on the day. I needed something unwavering to guide my view of self.

I looked to God's Word to start the process of discovery and couldn't believe how much I was missing about myself:

1. *You are set apart and accepted.* "You are the ones chosen by God, chosen for the high calling of priestly work, chosen to be a holy people, God's instruments to do his work and speak out for him, to tell others of the night-and-day difference he made for you — from nothing to something, from rejected to accepted" (1 Peter 2:9 MSG).

2. *You are wonderfully made.* "For you created my inmost being; you knit me together in my mother's womb. I praise you because I am fearfully and wonderfully made; your works are wonderful, I know that full well. My frame was not hidden from you when I was made in the secret place, when I was woven together in the depths of the earth. Your eyes saw my unformed body; all the days ordained for me were written in your book before one of them came to be" (Ps. 139:13 – 16).

3. *You were created for a purpose.* "For we are God's handiwork, created in Christ Jesus to do good works, which God prepared in advance for us to do" (Eph. 2:10).

4. *You are noticed.* "You have searched me, LORD, and you know me. You know when I sit and when I rise; you perceive my thoughts from afar. You discern my going out and my lying down; you are familiar with all my ways. Before a word is on my tongue you, LORD, know it completely" (Ps. 139:1 – 4).

5. *You are forgiven.* "When you were dead in your sins and in the uncircumcision of your flesh, God made you alive with Christ. He forgave us all our sins, having canceled the

charge of our legal indebtedness, which stood against us and condemned us; he has taken it away, nailing it to the cross" (Col. 2:13 – 14).

6. *You are a child of God.* "Yet to all who did receive him, to those who believed in his name, he gave the right to become children of God — children born not of natural descent, nor of human decision or a husband's will, but born of God" (John 1:12 – 13).

7. *You are loved.* "See what great love the Father has lavished on us, that we should be called children of God!" (1 John 3:1).

8. *You are made new.* "Therefore, if anyone is in Christ, the new creation has come: The old has gone, the new is here!" (2 Cor. 5:17).

9. *You are taken care of.* "Be content with what you have, because God has said, 'Never will I leave you; never will I forsake you'" (Heb. 13:5).

10. *You are redeemed.* "Christ redeemed us from the curse of the law by becoming a curse for us" (Gal. 3:13).

I couldn't believe how much God's Word spoke of my identity (and this list is only a glimpse into the truth found in the Scriptures). It spoke to the lies and labels that I had struggled with my entire life and brought healing to my insecurities, fears, and doubts.

But no matter how much truth I found, it was meaningless unless I was able to apply it. First, I had to learn to take hold of the thoughts and beliefs that were tripping me up, the ones that I kept defaulting to again and again. The human brain is wired to think, believe, and respond a certain way as a product of life's experiences. I like to call this the "default thinking pattern." Undoing that process requires deliberate effort. You have to figure out where your thoughts have taken a wrong turn so that you can get them back on the right track.

For me, journaling gave me the opportunity to find patterns in my beliefs and to recognize my default thinking. I encourage all of my clients to make their emotional world tangible with pen and paper. There is something undeniable about thoughts when they are staring you in the face.

Second, I had to replace my default thinking with God's truths over and over again. Each and every day, I caught myself defaulting to my old beliefs, resorting to my old labels. I had to stop myself and start over, seeking God's opinion over my own. The more time I spent digging into the Scriptures, the more good news I found and the more I was able to reclaim my identity and value, rooting them in the soil of God's crazy love and wonderful purpose for my life. Soon enough I came to realize that his purpose included my love life as well.

BECOMING MR./MS. RIGHT

When it came to discovering my identity and who God wanted me to be, I realized that a huge part of finding Mr. Right was in my becoming Ms. Right. I'm always telling young adults in my office to *become* the kind of person they want to marry.

> ### FAQ 6
> Do your career aspirations need to line up with your partner's in order to have a healthy relationship?

Are you looking for confidence? Then learn to be comfortable in your own skin and love yourself. Is communication important to you? Then become a person who learns to communicate with the people in your life. Are service to others and a concern for social justice things you want to see in your marriage? Then get involved with the right organizations and start making a difference as a single young adult. Become the person you want to spend the rest of your life with, because you will end up attracting those who are on your level and repelling those who are not.

DARREN'S STORY

After an ugly breakup, Darren was ready to give up on finding true love. It seemed to him that his entire life had been consumed by this search. He realized that he had lost himself in the pursuit of relationships, giving up a part of himself to every girl he tried to please. And he was left with a broken heart and a misplaced identity.

When I met Darren, he was at the end of his rope. The pain of broken relationships had severed his spirit and depleted his passion for life. Caught between the voices of his parents, his past relationships, and his college buddies, he wasn't sure who he was anymore. In his confusion, he had lost his appetite for living.

I challenged Darren to take a break from relationships and begin dating inward. It was time to become Darren again. It was time to take back the parts he had given away and invest in finding himself.

Darren did just that. He enrolled in school, something he had put off for quite some time. He followed his passion for justice and the law by taking classes to become a police officer. He invested in healthy friendships, attended church, and volunteered to help those who were less fortunate than him.

Darren finally understood that he had invested so much in finding and keeping a girlfriend that he had never focused on himself. He started doing things he loved and got to know his true self. For the first time in his life, his confidence was based not on the emotional roller coaster of relationships but on his God-created identity. His confidence grew, and his emotional health increased along with it.

Darren had to stand alone and learn who he was before he could join his life with that of another person.

HOW DO YOU LIKE YOUR EGGS?

Darren's story is the unfortunate reality of many young men and women today. So consumed by relationships, they never have the opportunity to stand alone.

A scene in a popular romantic comedy, *Runaway Bride*, depicts a woman in various stages of her dating life. When each man she is dating asks her how she likes her eggs, she always chooses whatever he likes best: scrambled, fried, poached, egg-whites only, and everything in between. She has no idea what she likes because she never takes the time to discover herself. She finds her identity in the man she is with rather than in the woman she is.

Although this is just a humorous detail in the film, I see profound truth in it. So many people have neglected to get to know themselves in exchange for the comfort and false security that a relationship may bring. They lose themselves in a relationship that ends up failing because they have failed to reflect their true selves. Not knowing who they are, they fail to recognize what they need.

Getting to know who you are sounds easy, but it takes some serious thought and time. It requires a genuine look into the fiber of your being, asking difficult questions and seeking the answers. More than simply figuring out how you like your eggs or identifying your favorite color, it requires much deeper self-awareness. It delves into the discovering of your personality, your likes and dislikes, how you prefer to interact with others, your values and worldview, your strengths and weaknesses, your flaws and talents, and even your day-to-day actions and reactions.

It's a process that is not accomplished in a day, a year, or any given period of time. It is a lifelong process, a journey on which you will find that there is more and more to be discovered.

Are you ready to take a look into the mirror?

Questions for Reflection

1. What positive or negative voices have shaped your identity?
2. On page 42–43 is a list of ten scriptural truths about your identity in Christ. Which of these do you struggle to believe?
3. What kind of people do you tend to attract or be attracted to? What does this reveal about your emotional health?

Application: Begin getting to know yourself this week by starting an emotional-health journal. Keep track of your thoughts, feelings, and beliefs about yourself, as well as your actions and reactions to the world around you. Spend some time reflecting on your observations.

Journaling Starter Questions

1. *Interactions and reactions.* What kind of people do I spend most of my time with? How do my interactions with them impact me? Are most of my interactions with others positive or negative?
2. *Behaviors.* What habits or hang-ups am I dealing with right now? Am I engaging in any addictive behaviors? What are some negative patterns I need to change?
3. *Feelings.* What is my overall mood throughout the week? What makes me sad? Angry? Irritated? How do I cope with negative feelings when they arise? Is this strategy healthy or unhealthy?
4. *Thoughts and beliefs.* What do I think about most? Do my thoughts reflect a positive or negative attitude toward myself? Are there thought patterns that I need to change? What do I believe about myself? Where did these beliefs come from? How do these beliefs line up with God's Word?

CHAPTER 4
WHERE AM I GOING?
A Vision for My Future

"Are we there yet?"

My parents will probably never forget the trauma my brother and I caused them on our many family vacations. But what's a kid to do? I remember epic road trips that seemed to have no end. Hours and hours of driving with no destination in sight. After we had eaten all the snacks, sung the same songs ten times over, and played games until we needed a referee to keep us from killing each other, things started to get ugly.

So what did we do to keep our sanity? "Are we there yet?" Every minute seemed like an hour, so it seemed perfectly fair to my brother and me to ask that question every couple of minutes.

Somehow my parents managed to keep their cool. As the driver, Dad always knew where we were going and when we would get there. As the navigator, Mom always reminded us that the end was near. They knew the way. They understood the journey. They were confident about where we were going.

The third component of dating inward is developing a vision for your life. After recognizing where you came from and understanding where you are, the rest is all about where you're going.

Proverbs 29:18 reminds us that "where there is no vision, the people perish" (KJV). Vision is the difference between maturity and immaturity. It's what separates the kids from the adults. My parents were able to keep their cool on those seemingly endless road trips because they had a vision. The kids melting down in the back seat, on the other hand, did not.

Vision will not guarantee success, but it will point you in the right direction and keep you from wandering into the kinds of relationships that you never intended to have.

SUSAN'S STORY

Susan had always had a vision for her life. Even long before our days as college roommates, she had a feeling that God was calling her to something far bigger than the American Dream. Her heart for the world was restless, but she knew that God would take her where he wanted her to go. There were many distractions along the way, many relationships that easily could have snagged her. But Susan knew her vision. She knew her calling, and she believed in a God who would fulfill that calling if only she continued to follow.

After college, she followed that calling to places all over the world, reaching people with God's love. As she witnessed the devastating effects of a tsunami during her time in Thailand, and as she endured the hardships of being a minority during a time of revolution and change in the Middle East, Susan remained faithful to the vision God had planted in her heart. And in due time, that vision brought rewards far greater than she ever could have imagined.

> **FAQ 7**
> How do cultural differences impact a relationship? •

During one of her mission trips to the Middle East, Susan met and fell in love with the man who one day became her husband, and she fell in love with the country that she soon called her home. God had a unique and extravagant plan for her life, and the vision he had planted in her heart led her to find true love and to marry a kindred spirit.

And not only did their shared vision unite them, it still keeps their marriage strong.

THE BIG(GER) PICTURE

My favorite part about Susan's story is that she wasn't out to snag a man. The vision that she was following was far deeper and much more permanent than the joys of a marital relationship. She was after the bigger picture, the calling that God had placed on her life. She knew that her life had a purpose and that pursuing God's will was the only way she could find true joy.

God is after the bigger picture of your life. He is writing your story. I'm about to say something that may seem antithetical to this book, but I need you to hear this: your story has far more to do with finding God's unique calling and purpose for your life than it does with finding the love of your life.

Did you hear that?

So many men and women come into my office broken and discouraged because their life's purpose is wrapped up in a relationship that has failed them or let them down. This is not the way God intended it to be. Finding true love may be a beautiful portion of your story, but it was never intended to be the grand finale. It's too easy to work so hard on this one section of our story that in the meantime the rest of the book never gets written. God's plans never play out in our lives because we are so fixated on finding love that we don't take the time to look at where we are going.

LONGINGS THAT SLAY LIVING

It was the end of my senior year in college. The previous few years had been somewhat of a roller-coaster ride in the area of romantic relationships. I found myself more preoccupied with snagging a man than I had ever thought I would be. I had always thought I would be married by age twenty-two (shows how much I knew), so it was now or never. It seemed as though time was running out for me and that the last year of college was my final opportunity to meet Mr. Right.

God had the grace to use one last dead-end relationship to get me to stop and take a look at the wannabe bridezilla that I was turning into. I realized that I had been so wrapped up in finding true love that I was missing out on so much of my college years, missing out on what was going on around me. I was missing out on friendships, the opportunity to learn, and the chance to capture my vision and the calling that God had placed on my life. Because I was so wrapped up in what I wanted, I failed to appreciate and marvel at what I already had been given. I needed a good dose of missionary Jim Elliot's beautiful reminder: "Let not our longing slay the appetite for our living."

That year I committed to God that I would pursue him and his vision for my life more than anything else. I wanted to be deliberate about letting go of my obsession with finding true love. He had promised that if I sought him with all my heart, he would take care of the details. I wanted to bank on this promise and decided to shift my focus upward. My feelings had been divided because of my longing for a future mate, but now it was time to make God sole proprietor of my affections.

A few months prior, I had volunteered to work in an at-risk inner-city neighborhood with one of the ministries at my college. I decided that this would be the perfect place to pour my energy into. There was something about that community and the children I met that had stirred my heart, and I felt God calling me.

One afternoon after class, I drove down to the neighborhood and parked my car on the side of a little street in the hope of running into some of the kids I had met the time before. I did, and they showed me around their neighborhood. I remember that as we walked around, I felt God's vision for my life growing stronger and stronger with each step.

I'll never forget that day, because that is the day that changed the direction of my heart and, in turn, my life. Rather than dreaming of the man I would fall in love with one day, right there and then I fell in love with a community of people. My visits to this part of town increased with each passing week, and before I knew it, God had given me an opportunity to partner with the city in starting a mentorship program for inner-city children. That year, Big Friend, Little Friend was birthed. What started as my friendship with a group of troubled youth blossomed into a mentoring program involving more than fifty people that was having a dramatic impact on the lives of the children, volunteers, and community.

Being the director of that program changed my life and brought me so much joy in the next few years. I loved every moment I spent with those kids, and the relationships that I built in that community are ones that I wouldn't trade for anything in the world. Following God's vision for my life allowed me a place to pour my affections into. Rather than save my love for the man of my dreams, I poured out the love God had given me into the lives of children who had never before had the opportunity to know love.

This vision for my life propelled me forward and allowed me to live each day for the joys that were before me, rather than just obsessing over the things I did not yet have.

CATCH ME IF YOU CAN

There's a saying that I heard as a young single woman that has had a profound impact on my life. I don't remember exactly where I heard it, but I do know that it rocked my world once I started applying it: "Fix your eyes on Jesus and the plans he has for your life. Look ahead, and run after him with all your heart. Then look around. Whoever has kept up with you, marry that person."

This saying challenged me to keep focused, to know my vision, and to look ahead to God's plans for my life. No distractions, no pit stops, no wrong turns. It wasn't until after I decided to pursue God's purpose for me that I eventually came face to face with the man of my dreams. As we were both looking ahead to God's plans for our lives, our stories collided in a miraculous and unexpected way.

BE MY VISION

I had just wrapped up a great school year as well as an incredible year with the Big Friend, Little Friend mentoring program. Summer break was calling me home for respite and refreshment, and lucky for me, my cousin Maggie would be crashing my home for some long-awaited summer fun.

A couple of weeks into summer, Maggie told me there was a guy she wanted to set me up with. But for the first time in a while, I was single and at peace with that status. Though I thought the prospect of meeting a potential boyfriend was interesting, we decided instead to head to the Boston area for an annual young-adult Christian conference.

That weekend was an awesome time of encouragement and growth, and I recall meditating on the topic of God's will for my life, since it kept coming up again and again throughout our sessions. I wanted so badly to focus on him, to capture his vision for my life.

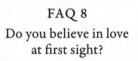

FAQ 8
Do you believe in love
at first sight?

But even while expending a great effort to focus, I kept noticing a handsome man out of the corner of my eye.

I was disappointed in myself for being so easily distracted. Here I was at this conference to reconnect with Jesus, and I couldn't stop my heart from wandering at the prospect of finding love.

I remember opening my journal that evening, determined not to write a word about that good-looking guy. (As if that would make him go away.) Instead, I meditated on the book of Hosea and journaled these thoughts:

July 2

Hosea 2:13: " 'She ... went after her lovers. But me she forgot,' declares the Lord."

I look in the mirror and I am consumed, even if so innocently — consumed with myself. I am the love of my life, living to please myself, living to impress those around me by my beauty, humor, spirituality, and good deeds.

And all the while, God is beckoning me to come. Come to my side ... come and meet me. And He pulls me into the dry desert, so that my wandering eyes have nowhere else to look but Him. And there, He speaks to me. There, He allures me with words of love. There, He reminds me that this world has so very little to offer ... and tells me that I am His beloved, and He is mine.

This is where the greatest joys can be found. Now, there is nothing worth glancing at, nothing worth aiming for, nothing worth investing in — except knowing Him more. That's what I want today.

This is not the kind of verse to which I typically would point someone who is pursuing a relationship. But should it be? In this verse lies the reason I was able to find true love. It required a vision and a steadfast focus. It required that I never forget my Lord in the pursuit of a relationship but rather always be in tune with him and the bigger picture he had in mind. It was when I finally captured God's vision for my life that I was able to recognize the kind of people who fit into my story.

All throughout the pages of my journal I found myself jotting down this reminder from an old hymn: "Be Thou my vision, O Lord of my heart. Naught be all else to me save that Thou art."

Little did I know that this reminder to keep my sights on my relationship with God and the plans he had for my life was the very thing that extended my vision far beyond my wildest dreams, eventually drawing me even closer to the man I one day would marry.

• • •

I hope by now you are starting to understand the importance of getting to know yourself. The answers to the questions, Where am I coming from? Who am I now? and Where am I going? are the truths that define who you are and will shape your future relationship. Finding true love starts with dating inward, long before you set eyes on anyone else.

So what are you waiting for? It's time to set a date with yourself.

Questions for Reflection

1. In your pursuit of getting to know yourself, have you discovered a vision for your future? What is it?

2. What does it mean that God would "be my vision"? Are you in tune with God and his bigger picture for your life?

3. What steps are you taking toward living your vision?

PART TWO

DATING OUTWARD

CHAPTER 5

DO YOU KNOW WHAT YOU WANT?

"Can I take your order?"

When it comes to ordering from a restaurant menu, there are two kinds of people. There are those who know exactly what they want within the first few minutes of scanning a menu. Decision-making is pretty easy for them, even while carrying on a conversation. They either always get the same thing or always lean toward a certain category of food that usually satisfies their taste buds. They choose what they want, casually close the menu, and sit back and relax as they wait for their order to be taken.

Then there are those who study the entire menu hoping for some sign as to what they should get. They ask their friends and the waiter (and some have even been known to ask other guests) for help in making such a difficult decision. They keep requesting a few more minutes before they finally decide, usually forced to choose because of the lack of time and the complaints of others at the table.

When it comes to ordering from a menu, picking a movie, or figuring out how to spend a Friday night, indecisiveness is not the end of the world, and it's okay if you choose poorly. Making the wrong decision may be irritating, but the consequences are not life shattering.

But when it comes to finding a life partner, not really knowing what you want can have devastating results.

I'm amazed by how many young men and women enter dating relationships without knowing what they want, much less what they need. For them, dating is like reading through an old-school "choose your own adventure" book in which they figure out the story along the way.

I don't mean to dismiss the fact that there are always a series of unknowns and the excitement of mystery when entering a relationship, but the unknowns should not be leading the way. It is important to know what you are looking for even before you enter a relationship. Too often people are catapulted into relationships by physical attraction or the thrill that comes when someone shows an interest in them. While this is natural, those who have not considered what they're looking for in a relationship may find themselves winding down an unforeseen path.

DENISE'S STORY

Denise was different from all the other freshman girls at her university. Her friends knew her as a mature young woman with a passion for God and a heart for people. She had always dreamed of the perfect relationship but had never really thought through what that entailed. She was just looking for a Prince Charming. New to college, to the world of dating, and to attention from the opposite sex, she fell fast and hard for the first guy who swept her off her feet.

> **FAQ 9**
> What does the Bible have to say about dating?

Ryan was definitely a Prince Charming. Born and raised in the South, he had the reputation of a true southern gentleman and a sweet southern drawl to match. She was swept away by his manners and his charm. He paid for her meals, walked her to class, and opened doors for her, and Denise felt like a princess.

As the months and years went on and their relationship unfolded, Denise started longing for something more. Sure, she loved Ryan's allure and the way he made her feel, but something seemed to be missing. The more she got to know him, the more it became obvious that they had nothing in common and that they were headed down separate paths. She longed for someone to challenge her, to sharpen her in her faith, to share her passions, and to propel her forward in life. But Denise felt trapped and obligated to stay in the relationship because of how much time and emotion she had invested in it. Thinking of starting over was just too much for her to bear.

She reminded herself that Ryan was a "good enough" guy. And he was. But unfortunately, all too often Mr. Good Enough ends up taking the place of Mr. Right.

WHAT'S THE PLAN?

An overwhelming amount of wasted time and conflicting emotions await people who don't think through what they are looking for in a relationship. Even more unfortunate are those who enter marriage with an ambiguous idea rather than a well-thought-out plan. It's amazing how much planning we put into all other important areas in life, yet how little goes into entering relationships with potential lifelong partners.

My husband and I have been planning a big trip for a milestone anniversary celebration. Given the amount of money we're thinking of spending, you'd better believe that we have spent hours researching, making lists, making phone calls, asking questions, and discussing what we want as we choose a destination. Anyone planning to spend a lot of money on a memorable trip would do the same thing.

If people put that much planning into a trip that will be here today and gone tomorrow, how much more should they invest in thinking through the qualities they want in a lifelong partner?

MAKIN' A LIST, CHECKIN' IT TWICE

I was grateful to have in my life the wisdom of an incredible woman who mentored me when I was a sophomore in college. She was my psychology professor, and something about her heart really captured my attention. One day I happened to run into her in the ladies' bathroom. It's always a little awkward to have any sort of discussion in the middle of a bathroom, but I knew I had to make my move.

I asked her if she would be willing to meet with me as my mentor. At that stage in my life and being so far away from home, I knew that I could really use some guidance. That day in the bathroom of the formaldehyde-scented science hall, an incredible friendship began that has profoundly affected my life and my relationships.

Sundi and I met every other week for lunch and a chat. We talked about college, careers, family, and friends, but inevitably we talked about relationships. I mean, seriously, what's a college girl supposed to do? It's a season in your life in which you feel as though relationships seep into every compartment. I knew I needed wisdom in making the right choices and in discovering who I was and what I wanted. And the more I knew about Sundi and the road she had traveled, the more I longed to learn from her experience.

One day Sundi shared with me something so simple yet so profound and crucial to understanding what you want and need in a relationship. She encouraged me to make a three-column list to help me define what I was looking for in a partner. She called it the Red, Yellow, Green List.

The Reds

In the first column, I listed the reds — traits that I would never allow myself to settle for in a partner. The most important thing to remember about reds is that *red always means stop*. If you don't hear anything else in this section, hear this: you cannot change reds. Too often we rationalize that negative traits can be changed or that we can overcome them with our love. But the truth is that traits in the red list are often the result of a lifelong series of decisions and ingrained patterns in another person's life that are impossible for you to change.

Everyone's red list is unique and reflects that person's experiences and desires. I would never attempt to write someone else's red list. But drawing on my experience as a professional counselor, I believe that there are certain reds that should make everyone's list. Here are just a few examples:

- Addictive behavior (drugs, alcohol, sexual sins, financial recklessness, etc.)
- Abusiveness (physical, verbal, emotional, or sexual)
- Dangerous and uncontrolled temper or displays of aggression
- Codependency or emotional dependency (see chap. 7 for details)
- Pattern of dishonesty or betrayal

My list of reds ran deep and reflected my experiences and wounds, and it was crucial to me that a potential partner not have any of these characteristics. In addition to the traits listed above, the following were some of the things that made my red list. I did not want a partner who

- was not a believer (not in a relationship with Jesus Christ).
- had negative relationships or a bad reputation with friends and family.
- did not have a heart for serving God and others.
- pressured me sexually.
- did not receive the approval of my friends and family.
- did not respect authority.

Again, remember that red always means stop. If you compare your potential partner with your red list and find that he or she has even one red trait, *do not* enter an intimate dating relationship with that person.

Let me clarify that though *you* cannot change another person's negative traits, God can, and I have seen him change red traits in the lives of many of my clients and friends, and even in my own life. Though God is able to change people, we must never enter a relationship assuming that the other person will change.

Healthy relationships are founded on who the relationship partner actually is, not on who they could become.

The Yellows

In the second column, I listed the yellows — traits I would rather my partner not have or unknowns that I would need to explore. The key thing to remember with the yellows is that *yellow means proceed with caution*. For example, you may need to discover, think about, and work through the following:

- Sexual history
- Family of origin issues and problems
- Communication deficits
- Unhealthy habits or behaviors

Again, everyone's yellow list will be different. Because not everyone has the same experiences, one person's yellow might be someone else's red, and rightly so. As a young Christian woman, I remember thinking long and hard about this list. Here are some of the things I came up with:

- Lacks involvement in and dedication to church
- Makes negative jokes or degrading comments
- Has a bad reputation among peers
- Lacks the ability to encourage and uplift me and other people
- Has low self-esteem and low self-confidence
- Lacks motivation, goals, and dreams

These were just a few of the things that I was really careful about, areas in which I proceeded with caution until I learned whether a trait was incidental or permanent.

When looking at your yellow list, ask yourself whether you could live with these traits if they remain unchanged. I find that couples who come to therapy ready to file for divorce after many years of marriage started their relation- ships with lots of yellows. Traits that are overlooked or ignored during the honeymoon phase become more acidic with each

> **FAQ 10**
> Why do I always find myself in unhealthy relationships?

passing year and slowly erode the foundation of a marriage. If not discussed, understood, and worked through before a couple gets married, yellow traits eventually can leave one or both partners feel- ing an enormous amount of doubt and regret.

The Greens

In the third column, I listed the greens. This is everyone's favorite column, the part of the list where you dream of all the traits you desire in a partner. The beautiful thing about this list is that it's not exhaustive; I guarantee you that no matter how long your list of greens, when you finally do meet the love of your life and the person that God has for you, you will be introduced to greens that you had never thought of and didn't even know you needed. It's exciting! Here are traits that were vital to me:

- Has a deep relationship with Jesus
- Communicates richly and interacts deeply with others
- Challenges me to be a better person and a better Christian
- Serves others
- Has a reputation of integrity and respect
- Has positive relationships with family and friends
- Has a prayer-filled life

- Is in tune with my morals and values
- Respects sexuality and honors it as I do
- Has goals and dreams but also supports my goals and dreams

It doesn't matter how long or short your Red, Yellow, Green List is. The important thing is that you have thought about what you want in a relationship partner and use this list as a filter in your decision-making process. If you plan before you begin your dating journey, you can avoid making quick decisions based on feelings and guesses.

MAJORS VERSUS MINORS

You may have noticed how very little time I have spent discussing the things that tend to make it to the top of people's green lists: physical appearance, body type, career, salary, education, hobbies, and so on. When it comes to finding true love, these are what I like to call the minors. Relationships founded on minors are destined for heartbreak and pain.

Please don't misunderstand me; I believe that the minors have their place in the big picture, but that place is small compared with the things that really matter. It's important to be attracted to your significant other; it's important to be able to connect on both superficial and deep levels; and it's important to have things in common. But these things are just the icing on the cake.

KEN AND SALLY

I recently met a sweet couple, both now in their seventies, who had twenty-one years of relationships done wrong under their belt, and thirty-seven years of relationships done right. Both of them had been in relationships in which they had focused solely on the minors and, as a result, experienced devastating marriages — one had been betrayed and abandoned, and the other had been abused. Following their divorces, they each had reentered the world of dating in their thirties with broken hearts and bandaged wounds.

Their mindsets had evolved during their seasons of suffering, and they each sought to fix their eyes on the things that really matter in a relationship. They were now more interested in the majors. Having tried it their way the first time around, they were committed to God's way.

Rather than looking for Mr. Tall, Dark, and Handsome, Sally was now determined to settle for nothing less than Mr. Loyal, Faithful, and True. Having been wounded by Mrs. Blonde, Busty, and Beautiful, Ken was fixed on pursuing no less than Mrs. Passionate and Pure. But more than anything, they each were looking for someone who loved God and loved others. They were looking at actions, not words, and for love, not looks.

When they met at church a few years later, they quickly fell in love. Though they were physically attracted, that wasn't what pulled them toward each other. Sally was overwhelmed by Ken's servant heart. He put her before himself and served others with all his heart. He loved the Lord and showed that love in everything he did. He made her feel loved, he made her feel heard, and he made her feel special — things she had never experienced in her previous marriage.

> **FAQ 11**
> I just started dating this really nice guy/girl. But I don't feel that head-over-heels feeling. What should I do?

Ken, from his perspective, fell in love with Sally's mind and heart. Her character and love for the Lord were more attractive to him than he expected. He spoke with joy of her gentleness and thoughtfulness, her ability to process her thoughts and then share profound truths. She showed him love like he'd never felt, because she chose to stand on his side, to encourage him, and to befriend him.

Thirty-seven years later, they are still happily married because they founded their relationship on things that really matter, traits they saw clearly displayed in each other long before they ever exchanged wedding rings. They chose to major on the majors and minor on the minors, and allowed their relationship with God to be the thing that drew them together and that keeps them together.

Not only are they happily married; they are overwhelmingly in love. Sally laughed about how just the other day, a friend caught her and Ken smooching in the aisle of the grocery store. I hope I'm still sneaking smooches from my husband in the grocery store when I'm seventy years old.

But this kind of marriage isn't founded on luck or good chemistry; it's founded on healthy choices and hard work. Unfortunately, Sally and Ken had to learn the hard way how to make those choices. They had to be devastated by divorce before they learned to fix their eyes on what really matters.

But not so for you. You don't have to go through the emotional devastation of divorce to understand what matters in a marital relationship. Thousands of others have traveled that difficult way, so why not learn from their mistakes instead of making them yourself?

Dating outward begins with knowing what you want. Those who know what they want save themselves from the hardship of relational U-turns, emotional dead ends, and interpersonal roadblocks.

Do you know what you want?

Questions for Reflection

1. Have you ever made a list similar to the Red, Yellow, Green List? If not, begin your list today. If you already have such a list, what could you do to improve it?

2. Have you ever settled for a relationship with someone who had red traits? What was the result?

3. In your dating experiences, have you focused on the majors or on the minors?

CHAPTER 6

TIMING IS EVERYTHING
The Seasons of Relationships

"Not to sound cliché but . . ."

I recently threw out a question on Twitter asking people to share words and phrases that are way overused in Christian culture. *Season* was at the top of the list: "There is a time for everything, and a season for every activity under the heavens."

Thanks to Ecclesiastes 3:1, it's no exaggeration to say that Christians love to use (and overuse) that word. At a ladies' fellowship I attend at church, it's pretty much guaranteed that the word *season* will be used at least five times each meeting.

"It's just a season of life."
"What an exciting season for you!"
"Don't worry; it lasts for only a season."

It's by far people's favorite word to describe a period of time or the duration of a specific experience.

I remember one of my college pastors giving a brief lecture on dating. He stressed the value of experiencing every season for a year with your partner before you even think about saying "I do." There is power in following this advice literally — together experiencing each of the four three-month periods in a year. But I believe that it is even more meaningful to look at dating as having four seasons figuratively.

What if we looked at the seasons of dating as a purposeful experience? What if each season played a part in preparing us to discover true love? What if we viewed each season as time to work through emotions, boundaries, conflict, and communication?

People ask me all the time how long two people should be friends before dating and how long it is appropriate to be in a dating relationship. The answers to these questions are different for everyone. Ask many different happily married couples how their relationship unfolded and you will likely get a number of different answers.

If we take the analogy of four seasons literally, a dating relationship would take twelve months, one beautiful year filled with highs and lows and thousands of new discoveries.

You may be rolling your eyes at the prospect of taking twelve months. "How old-fashioned," you might be thinking. In our world of fast-paced romance and internet flings, it may sound preposterous to put a timeline on love, especially one as long as an entire year. You might be skeptical. I'm sure you have a friend or relative who met a mate and married within just a couple of months, and who is living a perfectly happy life.

> **FAQ 12**
> The person I have a romantic interest in has told me that our friendship will only ever be just that. How do I deal with being "just friends"?

I also know such couples. But they are not the norm. Research on courtship indicates that couples who were together for a substantial period before marriage are less likely to divorce than those who rushed into it.

I agree that though statistics are important, they aren't everything, and there are always exceptions to the norm. But if dating is essentially a practice run for a lifelong marital commitment, why not take your time and be sure you know what you are getting into? Why add more risk factors than you have to? What do you have to lose?

Each season of dating offers a spectrum of discoveries that will lead you either one step closer to true love or two steps back. Each season illuminates potential risk factors and provides the opportunity to water and nurture the seeds of a relationship to see if they will grow and mature into a flourishing lifelong commitment.

A SEASON OF FRIENDSHIP

Before you enter the seasons of dating, I think it's wise to consider friendship as the first step toward a healthy relationship. Be friends for one season — three months — before entering a committed dating relationship.

One of the benefits of being in a friendship first is that you can learn many important things about a person before romantic feelings cloud your judgment. As tempting as it might be to skip this phase and jump straight into a romantic relationship, it's important to take the time to form a solid friendship, because that's what a good marriage is built on.

John's Story

John met Deb at a church conference one summer. He describes the moment he met her as "instantly falling in love." In fact, he called his best friend, who lived across the country, to tell him, "I've met the girl I'm going to marry."

John had been saving his heart for that special someone. He was selective in his dating endeavors and had never really been in a serious relationship. Even though his heart told him to just go for it with Deb, his head told him to wait, and he pursued a friendship with her after the conference was over. He called her, visited with her, and got to know her as he would any friend. He made sure not to lead her on with flirtatious language or touch, and he tried to get to know her as a person.

Five months into their friendship, his feelings for her grew stronger and stronger. Through their friendship, he learned so much about her, and with every passing day, she seemed to fit more and more into the mold of the woman he had always dreamed of marrying. Not only did he feel that he loved her, he truly liked her and felt that their friendship was ready for the next step. He asked her to enter a dating relationship with him, and she accepted. Their friendship was a solid foundation for a healthy dating relationship that eventually led to an incredible marriage.

I have to confess that this is my absolute favorite story about finding true love, because it's mine! John pursued me as a friend and took the time to invest in my life. During our season of friendship, we learned a lot about each other before we took the risk of entering a dating relationship. I see the fruit of that friendship, because we are still best friends and our bond grows stronger each day. I am so glad he took the time to be my friend, though I wasn't always so keen on the idea. Let me tell you why.

Deb's Story

I was officially done with relationships at that point in my life. I had recently had my heart broken, and I took the opportunity to clear my mind and heal my heart at a church conference in Boston.

I spotted John entering the room during one of the conference sessions, and instantly felt attracted to him. Something about him was genuine and transparent. I loved the way he interacted with people and his kindness toward all of his peers. Even more, I could see his love for God shining from every part of his life. But because I had recently been led on by a young man who had no intention of dating me, I was wary of relationships and decided to keep my feelings for John to myself.

As the conference went on, I got to know John a little bit more, and when the day came to part ways, I was thrilled when he asked if we could keep in touch. And we did. John made it a point to write me, to call, and to visit every now and again. We started off on a really good note and built the foundation of a meaningful friendship.

As the weeks and months passed, though, I felt confused. All of the guys I had known in the past had blurred the line between friendship and romance. They would say we were just friends but then try to get physical or call me sweet names. My heart always got sucked in way too deep. Many times I was left with a broken heart before a relationship even began. And as harmful as it was, that's what I was used to.

John was different. He was genuinely my friend. He was there for me when I needed to talk, he challenged me to become a better person, and we had fun together. No flirting, no pet names, no cuddling or sharing intimate feelings. Though I respected this friendship, I longed to know what the next step was, if there was even to be a next step. But through this process of building a friendship, more than ever I learned to trust God with my heart rather than carelessly giving it to a man. Because things didn't move as quickly as I was accustomed to, I had time to watch my feelings unfold and think them through. Because John and I weren't talking about our feelings at this stage, I had a lot more time to talk to God about them, something that I had never really done well before. I was — for the first time in my life — able to protect my heart and prevent my emotions from going too deep too fast.

A journal entry I wrote during that time reveals a lot about what was going on in my heart:

August 26
     Still thinking a lot about my friendship with John Fileta. I've been trying to sort my feelings out, but to no avail. All I know is that I look forward to talking with him tremendously, and that I could

even say it is one of the high points in my day. I can also say that his character is above reproach, and his love for God and passion for life are evident. We get along extremely well and our friendship has quickly become valuable to me.

So, I'm asking you, Lord, to determine my steps. I may plan my silly and uncertain plans, but Lord, you hold the key towards life and truth. Show me which way you'd have me walk in. Show John as well. Guide the longings of my heart in whichever direction you please. And give me patience to wait for it.

Five months later (which seemed like an eternity), John and I had a conversation about taking our friendship to the next level. We had taken the time to get to know each other through our friendship, and we both liked what we saw. We could see a future with one another, and wanted to take the next steps toward building that relationship. For the first time in my life, I felt a significant amount of peace about entering a dating relationship. Our friendship had played an important role in preparing us for dating.

> **FAQ 13**
>
> My friend and I seem to be developing romantic feelings for one another. I've heard that dating a friend of the opposite sex may be the best way to ruin a friendship. I really value our friendship. Is it worth the risk?

Years later, I still love my friendship with my husband. Though during the first few months of our relationship I might have been tempted to skip over our season of friendship, I can see the seeds of communication, respect, self-control, and straight-up fun planted during that time bearing fruit in our marriage today. As the philosopher Friedrich Nietzsche put it, "The best friend is likely to acquire the best wife, because a good marriage is based on the talent for friendship."

Since friendship is so crucial to a healthy marriage, take at least one season to form a healthy friendship before entering a dating relationship.

THE FOUR SEASONS OF DATING

A lot happens in a year. In the spring, rain showers the earth and new life slowly appears. In the summer, we experience the warmth of long sunny days. In autumn, the air cools and the leaves fall from the trees, preparing us for the cold months ahead. Then winter bites us with frost, and snow blankets the earth. So much transformation occurs during those twelve months. Likewise, a relationship undergoes lots of change during the four seasons of dating.

Spring

Spring is one of my favorite times of the year, filled with new life and growth. Budding flowers break through the cold hard ground and eventually blossom. The sun is so warm and bright that it feels as though it is shining for the very first time. Everything is fresh, everything is vibrant, and everything feels new.

In the seasons of dating, spring is the first season. At the start of any healthy relationship, both people experience feelings so strong it's as if they'd never had a romance before. New love, new feelings, new experiences. The heart stretches and grows. The mind, body, and spirit wake from hibernation, preparing for something new, something fresh, something good.

While strong feelings don't always lead to a healthy relationship and certainly aren't guaranteed to lead to marriage, I worry about couples who enter their relationship without the feelings that come with spring. It's important to be excited about your new relationship. It's important to feel a connection, an attraction, and a joyful anticipation of what's to come. The absence of those feelings and that excitement means something is missing.

Darla had just started dating Sam. On paper, he was everything she could have asked for in a man: strong, determined, smart, and funny with a hint of sarcasm. Most of all, he was really into her.

Having grown up together, Sam and Darla had a good friendship that had slowly grown into a dating relationship.

Darla enjoyed talking with Sam and spending time with him, but the more their relationship progressed, the more Darla realized that she did not have the feelings she ought to have. She really appreciated Sam as a friend and as a brother in Christ, but feelings of excitement, joy, and anticipation of a future with him never seemed to develop. No matter how hard she tried to convince herself that he was right for her, her heart felt numb to his pursuit. She began to wonder if something was wrong with her.

Darla is not alone. Time and time again young men and women tell me they are in a relationship with someone who looks "so good on paper," but the feelings just aren't there. Rather than being excited and full of anticipation, they feel apathetic and confused.

For some people, the problem stems from within. Fear of commitment and trust issues stunt their feelings. But for others, the lack of emotion is a sign that something is not as it should be in their relationship. Something is missing.

> **FAQ 14**
> How do I know whether I am struggling with commitment issues?

Afraid of leading Sam on, Darla decided to break up with him. Though Sam had many good qualities, she recognized that there were too many yellow flags and that the caution she felt prevented her from investing her heart. It was time to back off before she was in too deep.

Let me repeat that feelings are not the foundation of a relationship, but they are an important launching point. There will come a day when you are married and will have to learn to love someone even when you do not feel like it, but that time is not now. Spring is not the season for commitments; it's the season for discovery, growth, and exploration. It's the season when you have the right to say yes to the next step, but also have every right to say no.

Springtime in dating is a season to revel in new beginnings. When the time is right, you will find that your feelings, growth, and connection to each other will naturally propel you into the next season: summer.

Summer

No season is as polarizing as summer. Most people either love it or hate it. It's the time of year when either the sun is shining warmly on your face or you find yourself caught in an unexpected downpour. The flowers are in full bloom, gracing us with their beauty as well as attracting pesky little bugs. The days are long and hot, and the earth is a playground just waiting for us to come out and play.

I love summertime. I think I was made for the heat. (And since I have an Egyptian heritage, I probably was!) I bask in the sun and watch my skin tan perfectly within a few hours. My husband and I are both major beach bums and consider the perfect vacation to be spending time with our feet in the sand, reading good books and sipping delicious drinks.

My good friend Sarah, on the other hand, cringes at the thought of the summer heat. One particular beach trip, she spent the entire day hiding beneath an umbrella, layered in clothes to protect herself from the sun. Having seen the bright red lobster she turns into after just a few moments outdoors, I don't blame her. She hates the mosquitoes, the sunburn, and the crazy heat associated with summer, and she counts down the days until it's over.

The summer season of dating is full of paradoxes and forks in the road as the relational heat is turned up. By this point, a couple is spending a lot more time together than when their relationship started. It is a season of shedding your layers and exposing your true self to the person you are dating. Transparency is so important in getting to know each other. But it's also risky. It leaves you vulnerable. It forces you to trust, and to give at the risk of getting nothing in return. Many young men and women have been burned in the summer of dating because they have given their hearts and revealed their souls and had their offerings rejected.

MICHAEL'S STORY

Michael had been interested in Christie for a really long time. After they had been friends for more than a year, he finally risked asking her out on a date. After a series of dates, Michael began to trust Christie and, for the first time in his life, felt a strong desire to share thoughts and feelings with her that he'd never shared with anyone before. She was always caring and polite, but Michael began to feel that the relationship was uneven. The more he shared, the more she withheld.

One Saturday evening, while Michael was getting ready to pick Christie up for a date, she called. With a quivering voice, she told Michael that she appreciated all that he had given to her, but that the more he shared with her, the more she realized he was not the right one for her. She apologized for not ending it sooner and explained that she was just afraid to break his heart. Michael hung up the phone feeling more confused and alone than he had felt in a long time. He had risked so much, and he felt that the risks he had taken had led him to nothing.

But contrary to what he felt, the risks Michael had taken *had* led to something profound — confirmation that Christie was not the one for him. .

I, too, look back on the rejections that I faced in my life, and I am grateful to God for them. As painful as it is to get burned in the season of summer, it is exponentially worse to be burned after getting married.

Those who never enter the summer season of authenticity within a relationship may avoid the immediate burn of rejection. But they will never get to experience the honor of being loved for who they are. Use this season in your relationship to get real with your partner by asking the hard questions and sharing the answers with one another. Be authentic, because what you have to lose during this risky season is far less than what you ultimately have to gain.

WHO TURNED UP THE HEAT?

Just as the season of summer brings the joys of longer days, the summer season of dating finds couples investing more time and energy in each other. During this season, they experience stronger commitments, stronger connections, and stronger desires.

With emotional connection comes the heat of physical desire. Every touch causes sparks to fly. It's a season of longings that take root in the heart, mind, and body.

These desires in and of themselves are good and healthy. It's important to be physically drawn to your relationship partner. It's natural to long for closeness and physical affection. We were created to connect with others, and so we should not simply repress our desires for intimacy.

On the other hand, indulging in these desires prematurely can cause some serious relational damage.

For many couples, as physical temptation heats up, their physical relationship slowly becomes the foundation of their interactions. Everything they do together and every simple conversation they have leads down the same path. I'm not talking only about sex, either. A couple can fixate on the physical while never once having sex. A physical fixation can trap a couple in summertime, preventing them from developing a meaningful relationship.

No one should deny the physical attraction that comes with this season of dating. It's natural, it's healthy, and it's good, if kept in perspective. Rather than indulging in the physical heat, you must acknowledge it, be aware of it, and, most important, protect yourself from getting burned by it. (More on this in chap. 8.)

Fall

It is ironic that fall is one of the most beautiful times of the year. The leaves are losing their vibrant green, giving way to bright reds, oranges, and yellows. The world is painted with radiant color — while dying underneath. Trees enter dormancy, shedding their leaves. Plants stop growing, relying on stored energy to get them through the cold months ahead. Branches become bare, grass loses its color, and before you know it, the beautiful leaves that filled the sky are brown and shriveled on the ground below.

The fall season of dating is the most difficult season a couple goes through. Though the relationship may look beautiful to the distant observer, it is going through much change. True feelings, thoughts, ideas, and opinions are being exposed. Two very different people are learning how to interact with one another; the deeper they get into their relationship, the more they learn that they are not entirely the same. The emotions of spring and the passions of summer tend to become dormant as differences are revealed, opinions are assessed, misunderstandings occur, and conflict arises.

One of the first things I discuss when I sit down with a couple who has become engaged is to ask them if they have faced any sort of conflict. I always hope that the answer is yes, because the success of a relationship is determined not by a lack of conflict but by how well a couple works through conflict. Conflict is an important part of bringing two people together, but if it is handled poorly or avoided, it can pull them apart.

There are three ways to handle conflict when it arises in a relationship. The way you and your partner face your differences reveals important truths about your relationship and will either propel you into the next stage or hinder you.

1. AVOIDANCE

When it came to conflict, Rachel was an avoider. She was the eldest of six children growing up, and for the good of the family, she tended to stuff her feelings and desires. She was so accustomed to taking care of her younger brothers and sisters that neglecting herself felt natural and became the norm. She never really learned to take care of herself. When Rachel began dating Seth, she took that mentality into her relationship with him.

While Seth was a fun-loving, outgoing, nice guy, he had some rigid opinions on gender roles. Even though she didn't always agree with him, Rachel felt that it would be better for her to keep quiet about her needs rather than to start an argument, so she adopted his opinions early in the relationship. For the first few months, Rachel gave in to pretty much all of Seth's requests, whether or not she had the time or desire. She helped him with his schoolwork and cooked his meals, and Rachel felt at times that Seth viewed her as a beloved servant rather than as an equal partner.

Rachel continued to serve Seth, doing her best to avoid conflict. She stuffed her feelings and repressed her needs, and two years later when Seth asked her to be his wife, she agreed.

I met Rachel twenty-five years into her marriage. Rachel still hadn't learned to voice her opinions or needs, which made for peaceful interaction between the two of them. But deep down inside, Rachel harbored the seeds of bitterness and resentment toward her husband. She felt used by him throughout their marriage, but her fear of confrontation kept her from expressing her feelings; instead, she watered and nurtured those dangerous seeds.

Men and women like Rachel never had the art of healthy conflict modeled for them growing up. The needs and wants of others were always the priority, and they learned how not to rock the boat.

I agree that it is important to put others first. Scripture clearly asks us to consider others to be more important than ourselves and to serve and love others just as Christ served and loved us (Philippians 2). But we are not called to love others to our great detriment. Rather, we are asked to love others as we love ourselves (Matt. 22:39). Do you believe that you are worth that kind of love?

When we, like Rachel, find ourselves depleted because of a lack of self-care and self-respect, we cannot be of any aid to others. Christians in particular tend to confuse humility with self-neglect and self-deprecation. As C. S. Lewis so eloquently put it in a quote frequently attributed to him, "Humility is not thinking less of yourself but thinking of yourself less."

I attended a conference in which one of the speakers confessed to the crowd that he had a massive toothache. His dental appointment wasn't until the following week, but he had wanted to come to speak to us despite the pain. I will never forget that talk because the entire hour was pretty much a waste of time. Throughout his talk, this poor man continually winced in pain and kept apologizing for the noises and groans he made, which were affecting his ability to get his message across. The pain was driving him crazy, and as a result, he was unable to serve his audience the way he had hoped to.

Weird situation, I agree. But this is a good picture of men and women who repress their needs and live with pain to avoid conflict. When we live with unmet needs and unspoken desires, the pain building up inside eventually becomes too great to ignore. But the healthier we become as human beings and the more we invest in our needs, the easier it is to think of ourselves less and the more we are freed to love and serve those around us.

If you're afraid of conflict, use this season of dating to overcome that fear and to develop skills for resolving conflict.

2. AGGRESSION

Aggression is a form of conflict management that runs over anyone and anything standing in its way. This dangerous bulldozer is fueled by negative emotions and can manifest itself through negative words or even through harmful physical behavior.

Ironically, some of the most aggressive people are actually some of the most depleted. Though they are quick to express anger, they lack the ability to get below the surface and uncover their true feelings and needs. Anger is a secondary emotion rooted in fear, pain, frustration, or sadness. When a person can't understand and communicate such feelings, it's natural to overreact.

Jeff was like that. Everyone knew that you had to walk on eggshells around him. One wrong word and you would face his wrath. He sacrificed many relationships with family, friends, and loved ones on account of his aggressive behavior, the most unfortunate being his relationship with his wife. She no longer could tolerate his aggression and inability to communicate, and one day he woke up to find that she had packed her bags and moved out.

But even though he had such a hard exterior, Jeff was an extremely sensitive man. He cared about the people in his life, and it mattered to him what they said and did. His feelings were easily hurt. His insecurities ran deep, and the second he felt them rising to the surface, he masked them with his rage. It's easier to show aggression than it is to feel insecure. It's easier to push people away and to live alone than to be emotionally exposed and vulnerable. And when I met Jeff, that is exactly where his aggression had led him. He was completely alone.

Jeff had never learned to handle conflict in a healthy way. Rather than dig up unpleasant emotions and come face to face with his needs, he hid behind his aggression. Jeff never did this intentionally; in fact, he didn't even realize his tendency to run from emotion until he entered therapy and began uncovering his wounds and revealing his emotional needs.

Maybe you can relate to Jeff. Though you may not have lost all of your family and friends, maybe you are unsatisfied with the way you handle conflict. Aggression is a serious problem and needs to be handled in a serious way. Though there are different severities of aggression, the root is the same — fear, insecurity, and pain.

It's important to deal with aggression by finding a trusted mentor or a professional counselor to help you shed your anger and reveal the emotions that lie beneath. Only then will you be able to connect with the people around you and become the healthiest individual you can be.

3. ASSERTIVENESS

I teach a college course on interpersonal communication. It explores the dynamics of communication from the broad scope of global cultures to the narrow scope of individual patterns. I start the class by having students reflect on their family of origin and the influence that it had on their communication abilities. Then I ask them to respond to the question of whether they think they are avoidant, aggressive, or assertive in their interactions.

No matter what semester I'm teaching or who is in my class, a large number of students confuse assertiveness with aggression. The assumption is that a person who always says what they mean or gets their way is an assertive person, no matter how they go about communicating. The tendency is to believe that being mean, rude, or disrespectful is what it takes for a person to get what they want in life.

My favorite book on the topic of assertiveness is *Your Perfect Right* by Dr. Robert Alberti and Dr. Michael Emmons. In this book, the authors define assertiveness as "direct, firm, positive — and when necessary, persistent — action intended to promote equality in person-to-person relationships. Assertiveness enables us to act in our own best interests, to stand up for ourselves without undue anxiety, to exercise personal rights without denying the rights of others, and to express our feelings honestly and comfortably (e.g., affection, love, friendship, disappointment, annoyance, anger, regret, sorrow)."[2]

The most empowering part of this definition is the emphasis on acting in your best interests while continuing to respect the person standing before you.

Assertiveness is about equality, not power. It is about communication, not control. It offers an avenue for honest self-expression without devaluing the person you are expressing yourself to. It is free of manipulation, negative language, and intimidation. It's not only about what you say; it's about how you say it.

Miranda and Tony had been dating for six months. Having both been raised in families where open communication was not promoted, they decided early in their relationship to discuss things big and small in an open and honest way. They faced their differences and discussed their needs with one another, always creating an atmosphere of respect and working through conflict in a mature way.

But there was one issue that Miranda was never sure how to bring up. It seemed so insignificant compared with all the other great things about Tony. But the longer she tried to ignore it, the more hurt Miranda became, and the stronger she found her negative feelings growing.

Tony had a great sense of humor. He could always make people laugh with a witty comment or a sarcastic word. Miranda loved this about him, but there were times she felt that he crossed the line. Tony and his three older brothers were raised in a home where negative joking was normal. It was okay to call each other names or to put each other down for the sake of a good laugh.

But Miranda was hurt by some of his comments and jokes. She wanted to be honest with him but always found a way to talk herself out of having the conversation. One night after an exchange of jokes, Miranda felt herself emotionally pulling away from Tony. The issue was taking its toll on their relationship, and her silence was slowly drawing them apart. She decided it was time to communicate assertively, no matter what the outcome might be.

She made it clear to Tony that she loved his humor but that he had crossed the line and hurt her feelings. She explained her need for affirmation and the negative effects this kind of joking was having on their relationship. She reminded Tony that there were so many things she appreciated about him and that she hoped they could find a resolution to this particular problem.

Tony took Miranda's concerns seriously. He acknowledged his role in the situation and agreed that negative joking was of no benefit to their relationship. He could still be funny without putting her or others down, and he would try to do that from this day forward. He apologized for hurting her, and they committed to moving on together.

This issue may seem small, but even in solid relationships, it is the smallest of things that, when left unaddressed, take root, allowing bitterness and resentment to grow. Miranda chose to draw closer to Tony through her assertiveness, rather than allow passivity to drive a wedge between them.

The season of fall is about communicating, and communicating well. It is about allowing conflict to draw you together rather than tear you apart. It's about learning to deal with differences in a respectful and mature way.

Use this season of fall to strengthen your communication. Don't fear conflict; face it. Be open, be honest, be assertive, and allow this period in your relationship to stretch you, challenge you, and mature you, propelling you closer to finding true love.

Winter

Bundle up, because winter is here. If it were up to my husband, we'd pack our bags and move to the South around this time every year. To him, winter is a pretty insignificant season.

But others would disagree. I welcome winter because I see it as a forced settling of sorts. To me, it's that time of year when it's okay to stay home on a cold night. It gets dark at 5:00 p.m., and frankly, when the sun sets, so do my motivation and energy.

I particularly appreciated the winter when my first baby girl was born. As a new mother, it was nice to have excuses to stay home with my baby. "It's too cold." "They're predicting a huge snowstorm." "It's flu season, and I wouldn't want the baby to get sick." The truth was that after three months of sleep deprivation, I was just too tired to get up and get going. If there is ever a time to rest and relax, it's winter. It's a season for settling down and settling in.

Similar to the season of winter, when plants and animals settle in for the cold months and the world around them is muffled by snow, the winter season of dating is for the settling of emotion and the muffling of sentiment. In this season, your relationship slows into the normalcy of the day-to-day. The sparks of new beginnings have become a strong and steady flame, and the nervous energy of first dates has been replaced by the joys and struggles of life.

I love this season of dating. Though your emotions have steadied from their earlier highs and lows, they are still strong. No longer clouded by romance and infatuation, you have assessed your relationship in a clear light and found it to be healthy and strong. It is a time to admire what you have and to prepare for even greater things to come.

NO ORDINARY MONDAY

For John and me, getting engaged was an exciting time in our lives that we will always look back on with fondness. It was 8:00 p.m. on the evening of my birthday, which happened to be an uneventful Monday night. I pulled into my driveway after getting home from a Bible study, looking forward to talking to John for our nightly phone date.

I was living in Pennsylvania, and he was living in Illinois. The telephone was our lifeline during those months, and I couldn't wait to connect with him. Though we typically flew to see one another on special occasions like these, my birthday happened to fall on the day of John's first set of medical school exams. It was a rigorous day of seven hours of exams, and we had decided that it would simply be impossible for him to catch the last flight and make it out in time for my birthday. Instead, we planned to see each other in four days to celebrate over the weekend.

As I stood on my doorstep looking through my purse for my house key, I heard a car coming toward me. John and I were already on the phone, and at that very moment, he told me he had to go and would call me right back. Still scrambling to find my keys in the bottomless pit of my purse, I looked up to see an unfamiliar car pull into my driveway. The car door opened and my handsome boyfriend got out and walked toward me. It was like a dream. I couldn't believe it! There he was, dressed in a suit, with flowers in hand. "Hey, birthday girl!" he said calmly, with a huge smile on his face. In shock, I had to squeeze him just to believe he was actually there. He had managed to reorganize his day and catch the last flight so he could wish me happy birthday face to face.

I ran inside the house, put on my nicest dress, and we went out to dinner at my favorite place, the Hotel Hershey Circular Dining Room, where John had made a reservation for us. (If you haven't been there, you need to go. It will change your life.) We ate and then walked around the garden outside and enjoyed the beautiful fall day. It was like a dream. Moments later, John pulled out his journal and read to me the story of how he had fallen in love with me, a story he'd been writing about from the day we met. Shortly after, we both had tears in our eyes, and he got down on one knee and asked me to be his wife. (In case you're wondering, I said yes!)

The next morning he caught a 6:00 a.m. flight, and I was off to the daily grind at work, with a sparkling ring on my finger to prove that it hadn't been a dream.

IS IT NATURAL?

One thing that stands out to me during that time was the question I received from many of my friends: "What does it feel like to be engaged?"

I always responded by saying, "It feels natural."

Going from dating to being engaged should not be a life-changing, earth-shattering transition. As exciting as it was to be engaged, John and I had grown through the seasons of dating, climbing the steps one by one, and this was just the next step. It felt so right and made so much sense. For us, there was no other possibility and no greater option.

The winter season of dating prepared us for that step. It reminded us that day in, day out, our love ran deep and our commitment was growing stronger. It revealed to us that the infatuation of spring, the temptations of summer, and the conflict of fall had passed, and our relationship had survived, and it had thrived. We were able to keep our hearts close through the greatest test of all: real life. Winter was the opportunity for us to see what had been revealed through dating and to take those things into engagement and, ultimately, marriage. John and I loved what we saw, and still do today.

For some couples, winter is the season in which they find their relationship flourishing, not allowing the routine to hold them back but finding themselves connecting through it. They bear the cold, and the winter months pass smoothly, allowing them to enter into a season of engagement.

But it doesn't always happen that way. For others, winter is the season in which their love for one another begins to freeze through the long, mundane days and months. Rather than drawing together, they find themselves reflecting on what is missing and what has been lost. Unable to make it to the thaw of springtime, these couples part ways.

In the winter season of dating, take inventory of your relationship and make sure everything is as it needs to be before moving forward, because what you see in the season of winter is ultimately what you will get in marriage.

SEASONS COME AND SEASONS GO

Hopefully by now you've realized the importance of the seasons of dating. Though I've described these seasons chronologically, they don't always follow this order exactly. But the principles I've discussed are applicable throughout your dating relationship.

Just because you have been together for twelve months or more doesn't mean you have experienced all the seasons of dating because the amount of time it takes to pass through the seasons depends on how much energy you invest in them. Keep these seasons in mind as you go about your journey of finding true love. Be observant and self-aware throughout your relationship. Address your actions and interactions and reflect on what you are learning. Always remember who you are, and keep your wants and needs in mind.

Throughout the seasons of dating, keep evaluating your relationship. Is it natural or forced? Healthy or dysfunctional? Nourishing or draining? And if everything adds up — if you're sure you've found the right person and the timing is right — consider taking the next step into engagement. But be forewarned, marriage is a substantial journey, so choose the right person to come along.

Questions for Reflection

1. What can you do to set aside a season of friendship before starting a dating relationship?

2. Have you ever failed to protect yourself in the season of summer? What could you have done differently?

3. How do you tend to handle conflict: avoidance, aggression, or assertiveness? What can you do to improve your communication with others?

4. Have any of your relationships gone through the four seasons of dating? If you are in a relationship, which season are you in now?

CHAPTER 7

HOW TO PROTECT YOUR HEART
Emotionally Healthy Relationships

"To give, or not to give?"

She hung up the phone in frustration. The dial tone had signaled that she was no longer being heard. She couldn't even count the number of times their conversations had ended like this — in anger, arguments, and accusations. Why did he seem so distant, so unsure of their relationship? Why was it so hard for him to show her the love she craved? They had been in a long-distance relationship for more than two years, and she could no longer take the pain and stress of feeling so far away. She needed him to be close to her. She needed to feel him near — not just physically but emotionally. Maybe the distance was keeping him from giving her his heart. Maybe the miles between them were preventing him from letting down his walls. She had spent their entire relationship making excuses for him. She thought that if she just tried hard enough and loved deeply enough she could be the one to get him to change, to open up, to let go, and to give. Two years had come and gone, and she found herself in the same place she had started, feeling miserably and utterly alone.

YOUR EMOTIONAL TEMPERAMENT

This young woman is not alone in her frustration. Many people find themselves fighting a losing battle, trying to engage with an emotionally unavailable partner.

You may have encountered the term *emotionally unavailable person* in a psychology magazine, a counseling session, or even an episode of *Dr. Phil*. It's used to describe someone who refrains from investing emotionally in the lives of the people around them. Having been hurt in the past, or struggling in the present, they put up emotional walls to protect themselves from pain. Such barriers keep people at a distance, creating a false sense of security and control.

You might think that a person who has such major trust issues would never find someone to love and call their own. But at the other end of the spectrum is the *emotionally dependent person*. Having been hurt in the past by loss or abandonment, the emotionally dependent person fears one thing more than all others: rejection. Emotionally dependent people believe that they can get someone to love them if they give more, take less, and love better. And so they give and give and give to a relationship in which they are receiving hardly anything in return. When they feel that they've given everything they can, they give some more, hoping, praying, and waiting for love.

Emotionally unavailable people and emotionally dependent people attract one another and use one another to fill emotional voids. Though their needs are being met in unhealthy ways, relationships like these provide consistency, familiarity, and comfort, because for some men and women, the pain and struggle are all they've ever known. And being distracted by the flaws of the other means that you never have to focus on your own.

WE'RE ALL A LITTLE NEUROTIC

I'll never forget my first psychology class my freshman year of college. It was an advanced course in marriage psychology, and I was excited by the prospect of learning more about healthy relationships. I walked into the packed classroom and took one of the last seats in the room. The professor walked in with his bright green sports jacket and, in his robotic monotone voice, said nothing about healthy relationships. Instead he began to talk about how each and every one of us is in some way neurotic — neurotic, irrational, foolish, absurd, and disturbed.

I was taken aback and, to be quite honest, a little offended. I'd met some pretty neurotic people in my lifetime, but I felt that to say that I was one of them was going a little too far. But as the class went on, the professor slowly opened our eyes to the truth that each one of us carries some kind of baggage. Maybe it's something obvious like selfishness, irritability, or anger. Maybe it's something more subtle such as anxiety, fear, or doubt. But when we take an honest look into our minds and hearts, we will always find something that needs to be fixed, something that could use an adjustment.

As you read about emotionally unavailable and emotionally dependent people in the previous section, maybe you were tempted to tune out because you don't see either of these tendencies in yourself. But the key to discovering your emotional temperament is to look beyond the extremes to identify more subtle degrees of fear, rejection, and pain, feelings of worthlessness or pride, and tendencies to argue, control, or act aggressively. If we are honest, we will each find ourselves somewhere on the spectrum between emotional unavailability and dependency.

It's important to identify our emotional temperament because it has a big impact on one very important ingredient in relationships: our ability to trust.

TO TRUST OR NOT TO TRUST

When it comes to emotional intimacy, there are two types of people: those who trust and those who don't.

I worked in a counseling practice where one of the counselors specialized in treating children as young as eighteen months old. You might wonder what kind of counseling an eighteen-month-old could possibly need. The sad truth is that infants who have been abused or neglected (lack of food, shelter, touch) have difficulty connecting with people around them. Their negative treatment affects their capacity to attach, to interact, and to trust. This condition is referred to in childhood and in the teenage years as *reactive attachment disorder.*

From the moment we are born, our sense of security and ability to trust are shaped by our relationships, experiences, and interactions with others. Research has even linked early brain development and function to the giving or withholding of human interaction and response starting from birth.[3] A baby cries, and her father rocks her. She is hungry, and her mother feeds her. Through these basic interactions, she learns to feel secure and to trust others.

Our ability to trust continues to be shaped throughout our lives. Though we weren't able to control the impact others had on us at an early age, we can take control as we enter adulthood. Trust can be learned, and we can learn to let it be a trait that protects and nourishes us rather than causes us harm.

When it comes to the ability to trust, there are three kinds of people:

1. *Walls (emotionally unavailable).* Typically, walls are people who have been hurt by someone significant in their lives. Their ability to trust is limited because deep down they believe that no one can be trusted. Whether they experienced a few devastating interactions or a dozen less hurtful ones, they were left with emotional wounds that have

not fully healed. Having been harmed by trusted people throughout their lives, walls will do anything to protect themselves, even to the point of isolation. They build emotional walls in an attempt to secure safety, refraining from the give-and-take of relationships. Walls may be protected, but inside they are hurting, afraid, and enduring the pain of isolation.

2. *Free (emotionally codependent).* In the world of the free, there is no such thing as boundaries. "Come as you are" is their motto, because they will enter into relationships without hesitation. They love, believe, and hope even in the face of harm. You could say they trust people to a fault and ultimately pay the price by sacrificing themselves. Because they give people the benefit of the doubt, anyone is free to come and go as they please. And unfortunately, the free are bruised, betrayed, and misled time and time again.

3. *Fences (emotionally healthy).* It may sound harsh, but fences consider others to be guilty until they are proven innocent. But unlike walls, they are willing to let others in. They just expect people to prove themselves first. Fences see trust as a privilege to be earned, not a right. Rather than rely on a person's words and promises, they allow time, experience, and actions to reveal a person's character. Fences keep out the unknown and dangerous, yet open their gates to those who have demonstrated that they can be trusted. Fences are in a safe and healthy place.

Trust is essential to relationships and must be built the hard way. It requires time, experience, and love to grow strong. It is the result of a lot of hard work and dedication between two people. As one of my favorite quotes by author William P. Young states, "Trust is the fruit of a relationship in which you know you are loved."

It's important to recognize traits and patterns in our dealings with one another so that we can open ourselves to the prospect of being truly in love rather than just in need.

IN NEED VERSUS IN LOVE

You may not be aware of this, but true love has a dangerous rival, an opponent that disguises itself with passion, romance, and infatuation. It may appear that this love is the same as true love, but when you really get down to the roots of each kind of love, it is unmistakable that they are opposites. That rival is called "need." True love is founded on sacrifice, honor, selflessness, and respect (1 Corinthians 13). It is rooted in giving. But "need love" is all about taking.

Many who feel that they have fallen in love eventually realize that they are really only "in need." Their relationship is purely meeting a need in them — a need to be wanted, valued, affirmed; a need to be taken care of, nurtured, safe. "Need love" drives you toward another because of your disparity. It binds you together in codependency and unites you in fear. Need love fools two empty people into thinking that they can fill one another up. But in the end, fulfillment never comes. They feel more and more depleted, and their needs grow even greater in the shadow of this false love.

True love, because it is birthed by sacrifice, is never based on need. Because it is a choice, it's a love that exudes permanence and unconditional positive regard. It loves even when it doesn't feel like loving, and it gives until it can give no more. It loves the other person because of who they are, yet continues to love because of its nature. It is an unrelenting, passionate, fierce, and growing love that loves for the sake of loving; it loves to love, rather than loves to be loved. It wants nothing from the other but the opportunity to love them better.

A BETTER LOVE:
EMOTIONALLY HEALTHY RELATIONSHIPS

Nothing is more meaningful than being in a true love relationship. Emotionally healthy relationships allow true love to take root because they are founded on trust. But how do you establish emotional intimacy in a healthy way?

I heard a story about a bachelor who did some work on his house. The electrical outlets needed to be fixed, and though the bachelor had little electrical experience, he decided to save a few bucks by tackling the project on his own. He assumed he could learn as he went. But electricity had other plans. The bachelor underestimated its power and was ill-prepared to work with it safely. His ignorance of and lack of respect for electricity left him with major second-degree burns.

Before you begin to work on having emotionally healthy relationships, it's important to understand the power of emotional intimacy. More powerful than a kiss and more seductive than an embrace, emotional intimacy can supersede the bond of physical intimacy.

Earlier we discussed the importance of being genuine in a relationship, of revealing your true self. A problem arises, though, when you unveil yourself too quickly. It's like jumping into the deep end of a pool before you have learned to swim. The initial rush of emotion may feel good, but soon your lack of skill causes fear and panic. You cling to your relationship partner to stay afloat, not knowing whether they can be trusted. Jumping into deep emotional waters creates a dependence that binds you to your partner out of need.

But when a relationship is built slowly, the giving and taking of emotions between two people is earned in a slow and steady way. It's an unrushed process of learning to trust one another in the shallow end before steadily moving into the deep end. This results in a level of trust and commitment with your partner that never could be reached any other way. The emotional deep end becomes a sacred place of connection instead of desperation. You stay afloat because you have taken the time to develop the skill to do so. Without fear, you are able to love freely within the give-and-take of emotional intimacy.

EMOTIONAL DO'S AND DON'TS

Building trust in a slow and steady way involves establishing emotional boundaries — a set of do's and don'ts that guides you through the exchange of emotions without going too deep too fast.

Emotional boundaries can be difficult to establish. It's easier to put boundaries on physical intimacy — hands kept to a certain place, kissing kept to a specific limit. When I was in college, there was an ongoing joke about the Three-Second Hug Rule. If you were caught hugging longer than three seconds, your peers would call you out for having entered the realm of the inappropriate. Sometimes pesky onlookers even counted out loud for you so you wouldn't lose track of time.

But how do you gauge when emotional intimacy is pushing the limits? How far is too far?

Though I don't claim to have all the answers, God really challenged my heart on this subject during my season of dating. Reflecting on my dating history and on my clients' experiences, I have found that couples who develop emotionally healthy relationships usually keep the following boundaries in mind.

Guard Your Heart

If you're like me, you cringe whenever you hear the phrase "guard your heart." It's a cliché in Christian circles that carries a great concept but comes with very little practical application in that no one really knows how to put it into practice.

Guarding your heart means protecting the deepest parts of who you are — both your emotional and spiritual worlds — from anyone who could cause them harm.

Matthew 7:6 warns, "Do not throw your pearls to pigs. If you do, they may trample them under their feet, and turn and tear you to pieces." Sometimes people can be insensitive and uncaring. It's important to hold on tight to the things that matter to you until you know that you can trust someone. Don't be too quick to share your life story, your every thought, or your deepest secrets. Don't commit to praying for hours on end with someone you've just met. Prayer is a time of exposing your heart and getting emotionally naked before the Lord. Talk about an intimate moment.

It's vital to pray about your relationship and to seek God's voice for direction, but make sure you wait before you seek it together. Pursue God individually so as not to allow your spiritual relationship to become a trio prematurely. Not only is it okay to wait, but it's important to do so until the timing is right, until you have clarified your commitment, established trust, and experienced give-and-take in your dating relationship. Don't go too deep too fast, because emotional intimacy can pull you far deeper into your relationship than you ever meant to go and, in the end, leave you with the double damage of a broken heart and a broken spirit.

Guard Your Time

Naturally, two people getting to know each other in a dating relationship have a strong desire to spend time together. Being together seems like the natural route of relationship building, and so many couples try to maximize the amount of time they invest in one another, not realizing that there is great benefit in physical distance. Just as crucial as spending time together is spending time apart.

Time apart reveals so much about a relationship. The independence it allows will later translate to interdependence — two independent individuals choosing to rely on one another. Couples who spend an unhealthy amount of time together may become enmeshed, losing their independence. Be cautious of the emotional entanglements that can arise when two become one prematurely by investing all of their time into a relationship.

Set aside quality time for your relationship, but be sure to set aside quality time for yourself — for your relationship with God, your ministries, your hobbies, your family and friends. You were never meant to lose yourself within a dating relationship; rather you were meant to enhance yourself.

SAYING GOODBYE

John and I had been dating for a little more than a year. In the depth of our hearts, we both believed that we had found our perfect match and that engagement was probably right around the corner. Yet even with such strong feelings, we made it a priority to interact with each other in a manner that would leave us with few regrets if things didn't work out.

Having few regrets meant fulfilling the vision we each had for our lives. We were careful to allow one another to remain obedient to the individual callings that God had for us, even when doing so required sacrifice. John was in medical school, pursuing his dream of becoming a doctor. At the same time, I felt a strong leading toward mission work and had previously committed to serve in a third world country for two months. As the day approached for me to leave on my trip, I began to feel a little uneasy. My relationship with John had developed so strongly, and thinking of being away from him for two months was almost too much to bear. Deep down I knew that God had a great purpose for my trip

> **FAQ 15**
> Speaking of guarding your heart, is it okay for a woman to make the first move?

and that he would bless me for trusting his plan. But even so, I found myself hoping that John would ask me to stay, giving me a reason to cancel my trip so that we wouldn't have to be apart.

Instead, John consistently encouraged me to go. He affirmed his love for me and pushed me to pursue the plan that God had called me to, a plan that was established long before we had ever met. John promised me that he would be there when I got back, and then he handed me a present as we shared one last moment together.

John had put together an album of photos of our greatest memories from the past year. As exciting as that was to have, the most meaningful part of his gift was the note he had written on the first page of the album:

My Deb,

Words cannot even begin to describe how amazing my life has been since God brought you into my life. It has been so incredible to see God's hand at work in us, how much we have changed, how much our friendship and love have developed over the past year. You truly are the greatest blessing I have ever experienced in my life....

As you go to Egypt, as I go to medical school, as we walk together through life ... may we be reminded of God's faithfulness in our lives, and may it point us to the cross, waiting expectantly on God's will for our lives and for our love.

You wrote so perfectly to me before, "Even in the struggles of love ... of missing you ... of longing to be near you ... of having a constant aching in my heart ... Lord, Thy will be done. In the uncertainties of the future, of medical school, of occupation and location, of dreams to get engaged, and longings to be united for life ... Lord, Thy will be done. Learning to accept and bask gladly in the will of God NOW will teach us to always live at rest in His will hereafter. We are learning such amazing lessons, even through the struggles of being apart. God is affectionately loving us, and showing us His love through these times. He is reminding us that His grace is sufficient, that He is strong when we are weak, and that He can be trusted."

Praying for you every day, and falling deeper in love with you with every moment together ...

Go with me, my Love ...

John

And with those final words in our minds and hearts, we said our goodbyes.

The time we spent apart was difficult, but it taught us important truths about our relationship. Beyond the fact that it strengthened our communication, commitment, and affection for one another, it showed us that we had the strength to function apart. We were independent people, each with a unique calling and purpose in life. God was using each of us apart, preparing us to one day be used together.

One short month after my arrival home, John proposed to me, and we were married nine months later. Even to this day, the emotional boundaries we set during our season of dating continue to have positive effects on our marriage. Those boundaries protected us from codependency, allowing us to be the individuals God had called us to be. We continue to live out that individuality within the context of our marriage, because in true love, we are offered the freedom to be ourselves.

Spend time together, but also give yourselves the opportunity to spend some time apart.

Guard Your Mind

Any counselor will tell you that there is a reputable kind of therapy called *cognitive behavioral therapy*. The idea behind this method of healing is that how you think has a direct impact on how you feel. All through the Bible, God reminds us of the power of the mind and the repercussions of our thinking. We are told to renew our minds (Rom. 12:2) and to keep our minds focused on what is good (Phil. 4:8). For many people, even more significant than their external behavior are their internal musings. Consequently, our thoughts about dating can have a tremendous impact on our emotional world.

MOLLY'S STORY

7:51 a.m.: the slamming of the hallway door of Molly's college dormitory woke her suddenly. In panic, she looked at her alarm clock and jumped out of bed, wondering how she could possibly have overslept. She had an 8:00 a.m. final, and the professor was adamant that any latecomers would be failed.

7:55 a.m.: disheveled and running with one shoe still in hand, Molly went out to the street and frantically waved at passing cars, hoping to see a familiar face and catch a ride. Suddenly a car slowed down and the driver called for her to come on in. It was that gorgeous guy from her anatomy class! Could this be? He actually cares! Maybe this whole debacle was just part of God's plan to set her up with her soul mate.

They exchanged names and made small talk during the three-minute car ride — about the weather, about their college experience, and about their anatomy class. He told her he appreciated the questions she had asked after the last lecture. She was over the moon. He actually remembered? What could this mean for her? What could this mean for their relationship?

Though she got to her final just in the nick of time, her mind was elsewhere. She just couldn't stop thinking about the encounter.

THE DISEASE OF OVERANALYSIS

It's amazing the games your mind can play when your guard is down. Molly let her thoughts take over, and she spent the following weeks obsessing over and analyzing her encounter with this young man, who most likely never thought about her again.

I've met so many men and women who allow their minds to imagine a world that doesn't exist. Overanalysis causes you to make something of nothing, preventing you from seeing things as they really are. Hours spent picking events apart, reading between the lines, and dreaming of what could happen can occupy your thoughts and consume your time, immersing you in a world of dreaming that prevents you from experiencing real life.

It's important to guard your mind when it comes to love. Don't allow relationships to consume your every thought. During my dating years, I constantly repeated this verse from 2 Corinthians 10:5: "We take captive every thought to make it obedient to Christ." Focus on what God is doing in the here and now and align your thoughts with his. Home in on what is actually happening in your relationships rather than on what you wish to happen. Keep your thoughts in check, and your emotions will follow suit.

Guard Your Conversation

It is so tempting to talk about the future when you're dating. You want to dream together, to envision the future and create a life to live for. While it's important to be on the same page in a relationship, I've met far too many couples who have jumped into these kinds of conversations way too fast. Discussions about marriage, children, and even sexual intimacy should be delayed until after you've laid a foundation of commitment and trust.

It's a problem when you commit to the future before you've committed to the present. Rather than allowing your hopes for the future to blind you, savor, assess, invest in, and engage in your relationship where it is now. Commit to the moment, allowing your relationship to mature before permitting your conversation to jump ahead, because wherever your conversation goes, your heart will always follow. First lay the foundation; then build the house.

LEVELS OF COMMUNICATION

To gauge what degree of openness is appropriate in the development of a relationship, it's important to understand that there are three levels of communication.

In the first level of communication, the focus is on sharing facts. Conversation at this superficial level can be carried on with a stranger with little or no risk, because talking about topics like the weather, last night's football game, or the cafeteria menu reveals little of the self.

Level 2 conversation is a little more intimate, revealing more of the self as you express opinions and ideas. Rather than talking only about what happened during last night's game, you offer your opinions about the game and share your thoughts about your favorite team. Instead of just talking about the weather, you talk about your favorite season and share your favorite autumn moment.

> **FAQ 16**
> What are some questions that I can use to get to know someone better at the three levels of communication?

Level 3 is the most intimate level of communication because it reveals the deepest part of a person — the heart. At this level, conversation involves expressing feelings and opening up about struggles, joys, and fears, as well as sharing hopes and dreams.

The most important thing to remember about the three levels of communication is that they are progressive. They reflect the slow and steady deepening of communication as trust is earned. You may use them as a guide to help you protect your emotional world, as well as that of your significant other.

Your emotional world is one of your most intimate parts, so don't allow it to be compromised. Healthy dating relationships call for an accurate understanding of your emotional temperament as well as the gradual building of trust. Protect yourself by guarding your heart, your mind, your time, and your conversation. Take control of your relationship; otherwise, it will take control of you.

Questions for Reflection

1. Are you a wall, free, or a fence? What factors affect your ability to trust?

2. What are some ways you may have crossed emotional boundaries in your dating relationships?

3. In your relationships, do you tend to give or to take? How can you balance give-and-take? How can you move from need-based relationships into love-based relationships?

CHAPTER 8

WHY SEX MATTERS
Physical Boundaries

"Say yes to sex."

It's too bad we don't hear that more often in the church, because the glorious reality is that we were created with the capacity for sexual connection. It's a serious problem when Christians try to tackle the topic of sex as though it's a "say no to drugs" campaign, because there is so much more to it than that. We were never meant to say no to sex.

We were never intended to say no to sex because it is one of God's most valuable gifts to human beings. God is the creator of intimacy, and in his love for us, he bestowed this beautiful gift in which two people unite in the commingling of body, soul, and mind. We were never intended to say no to sex, but it's important to understand when to say yes.

THE HIGHS AND LOWS OF SEX

Few experiences are more intimate than marital sex. It's an act between two people that is intended for pleasure. God himself, through Scripture, invites us to fully partake in this sacred experience: "Eat, O friends, and drink; drink your fill, O lovers" (Song 5:1 NIV 1984). We are to indulge in it and enjoy it. It is a glorious connection, fusing the bodies and souls of two people in a mysterious and magnificent way.

Not only is marital sex the experience of deep intimacy between two people, it is also a reflection of intimacy between God and his people. Sex in its truest form is an act of love, selflessness, and service, all within the context of full human exposure.

But without a doubt, the inappropriate use of this gift is leaving millions of young people feeling more broken and alone than they ever thought was possible. I meet with young men and women and receive emails from people all across the country who are feeling the devastating effects of a premature sexual bond.

There are countless reasons why young people engage in sex outside of marriage. In some cases, sex is a physical substitute for unmet emotional needs and a cover-up for deep insecurities. In other cases, people use it to gain control and power in a world where they feel out of control and powerless. For some people, it's a moment of pleasure in a world filled with pain, brokenness, and agony. But for others, it's simply a God-given desire that has spiraled out of control to the point where they have grown numb to their convictions. But whatever the reason, the outcome is always the same. Because sexual intimacy is such a deep form of connection, it can cause even deeper wounds.

JUSTIN'S STORY

When I met Justin, I could tell right away that there was something authentic about him. He was the kind of young man who wore his heart on his sleeve. He had sought counsel regarding a broken relationship that had left him wounded and unsure of the next steps for his life. Watching his face as he told his story, I had little doubt that he was hurting and confused.

He described his romance with Bekah without pausing, reliving the memories of their relationship with each word he spoke. They had quickly fallen in love with one another after being introduced by a mutual friend, and from that moment on, not a day went by that they hadn't interacted in some way.

Their emotional intimacy had spiraled out of control, and their physical connection soon followed. They began compromising in small ways, staying up late to spend time with each other or falling asleep in each other's rooms. Within a few weeks, their relationship had become sexually intimate, and it remained that way.

The following months proved to be some of the most difficult they had ever experienced. Having given each other the emotional and physical privileges of marriage, they bonded intimately. They felt married, though they had never even been engaged. Soon enough the deficits in their relationship surfaced: communication issues, unhealthy conflict, codependency, jealousy, and rage. But their sexual intimacy gave them the connection and security they needed to fool themselves into thinking everything was okay.

They closed their eyes to the problems in their relationship until Justin could take it no longer. After two long years of their toxic relationship, he finally called it off. He couldn't imagine living without Bekah, but the pain was finally excruciating enough to let her go. With tears in his eyes, he told me of the wounds he had experienced and his feeling that he had been through the agony of a divorce.

Maybe you can relate to Justin's story. Maybe you are one of the millions of well-intentioned young adults who have found themselves in an unexpected place because their committed relationships have taken a turn down the road of sexual intimacy.

Whether you are dating, engaged, or just fooling around, sex outside of marriage causes devastation in your life and in the life of the one you love. Though there are many reasons why sex outside of the commitment of marriage can harm a relationship, I'm going to focus on some of the main problems I have witnessed as a counselor.

SEX COVERS RELATIONSHIP FLAWS

No matter what you call it, the season before marriage is an important time of life. It is the coming together of two people in an effort to know and be known. It is a trial period in which a couple pursues connection in the hope of discovering compatibility and making a lifelong commitment. That is some serious stuff. As exciting and exhilarating as this season can be, it's also loaded with pressure. But pressure can be a good thing.

The best analogy I've heard regarding relational pressure is from *Intimate Deception* by P. Roger Hillerstrom.[4] Hillerstrom compares a couple's relationship before marriage to a steam pipe. The role of this pipe is to transport pressure. But steam pipes are prone to cracks and imperfections. When pressure builds, these cracks and imperfections are revealed and can be repaired. But when pressure is released prematurely, it doesn't build, and the cracks are never found. And, Hillerstrom writes, "Eventually they'll corrode and destroy the pipe."

Every relationship must undergo healthy pressures to develop intimacy and discover what it's really made of — the pressures of family of origin issues, expectations, roles, personality differences, and the list goes on and on. Communication is the key to repairing the relational cracks revealed by these pressures. As a professional counselor, I can't stress enough the importance of building a marriage on healthy communication. As was the case in Justin and Bekah's story, one of the problems with sex outside of marriage is that it allows for pressure to be released through the physical, preventing cracks from being repaired through healthy communication and emotional exchange. Problems remain undiscovered or ignored until it's too late and what could have been an indestructible relationship has been destroyed.

SEX BREEDS GUILT AND TRUST ISSUES

I don't know many young men and women who profess to be in a relationship with Jesus who don't struggle with feelings of guilt and shame linked to premarital sexual intimacy. I have even seen these harmful feelings take root in the lives of young people who do not profess to be in a relationship with Jesus.

I've heard people argue that this guilt is the by-product of a legalistic Judeo-Christian belief system rather than a God-given conviction. But in my clinical opinion, healthy guilt is usually a sign that something is not as it should be, that something needs to change.

If you believe that God speaks through his Word, there is no getting around the fact that sex outside of the commitment of marriage is forbidden in Scripture.[5] Forty-four times in Scripture the word *porneia* (referring to sexual expression outside of marriage) is prohibited. It makes sense that the designer of sex might place limits on it. God knows what the misuse of this precious gift will do to his people, and out of his love for us, he wants to spare us unnecessary harm.

No matter how hard people try to justify premarital sex, many young Christians who are sexually active outside of marriage find themselves struggling with some really negative emotions (whether toward themselves or their partners). They are enmeshed in a supernaturally binding act (1 Cor. 6:16 – 17) without a commitment to the permanence of the relationship. This lack of commitment breeds fear, confusion, and even a deep sense of loneliness. Feelings of distrust and blame creep into the relationship, ultimately driving two people apart through the very act that was designed to bind them together.

The bitter irony is that by indulging in sex outside of marriage, you are actually robbing yourself of serious joys. Within marital sex, there is unlimited freedom and "unrestricted pleasure."[6] Doing it any other way produces guilt that, like a drop of ink, ultimately taints the experience. God wants you to revel in the gift of sex without a hint of shame, to be permanently bound together by its force, and to see it as the lavish gift that it was meant to be.

SEX LEADS TO FALSE INTIMACY

Many times I hear couples describe their sex life using the word *intimacy*. The truth is that it's a word that the average person takes lightly, often referring merely to a passionate sensation between two people.

Sex outside of a permanent relationship leads to false intimacy because it allows the couple to feel a moment of closeness that doesn't do justice to real intimacy. I've heard the word *intimacy* defined using the phrase "into me see," the act of taking off your mask and revealing your true self to the person standing before you, mind, soul, and body. Intimacy is so much more than a passionate feeling; it is commitment, revelation, knowledge, and pursuit. One thing these words have in common is that they all imply a long-term connection. They are most meaningful when they are used by those who choose to grow closer in love each and every day of their lives.

Sex is the physical means of expressing this kind of lifelong commitment between two people. It is the embodiment of ultimate security and sacred unity. It should be the product of true intimacy, rather than the foundation upon which intimacy is built.

SEX BREEDS HARMFUL EXPECTATIONS

Pick up any psychology textbook and you're likely to run into the concept of *imprinting*. Imprinting is the process during which animals after birth fixate on their experiences to the degree that they bond with their caregivers. Google the word *imprinting* and you're likely to find adorable pictures of a zookeeper or researcher being followed around by a line of Mallard ducks who imprinted on him after birth.

Recently this concept has been applied to human sexuality. In his marriage ministry to thousands of couples across the nation, Mark Gungor suggests that sex before marriage can imprint experiences on your sexual palette. Once those experiences have been imprinted, your body becomes sexually aroused only in those kinds of situations. He explains that "those who have their first sexual experience outside of marriage imprint on the lust of illicit sex."[7] When this happens, sex within a relationship becomes focused on simply recreating an experience rather than connecting with a soul mate. Fixating on recreating an experience robs sex of its innate thrill, and one's level of arousal becomes dependent on the situation rather than on the person.

Whether or not sexual imprinting is a reality, one thing is certain — sexual expectations are always based on sexual experiences.

Couples who engage in sex within the context of marriage find that their sexual expectations are based on a fixed situation: engaging in sex with the same partner in a lifelong marriage commitment. The permanence of this situation creates the need for creativity, ongoing growth, and deepened intimacy. But couples who engage in sex apart from marriage set themselves up for sexual expectations that are not based on a fixed situation, and therefore may not be met.

> **FAQ 17**
> Can my sexual past affect my future relationships?

The expectations created by sex outside of marriage are in flux because dating, by it's very nature, is a stage of transition rather than permanence. The relationship will either end in a breakup or progress into marriage. Expectations that are established during such a transitional period are based on a variable that ultimately will change, making it impossible to continue meeting sexual expectations that were set in the past. Your sexual past will always affect your sexual present because each experience before marriage adds to the mental, emotional, and physical description of what you expect out of sex. These expectations will affect your marital sex life by placing demands on you or your spouse that can no longer be met (since they were based on a transitional relationship that has ultimately changed), causing stress, shame, and emotional or even physical withdrawal. Saving sex for marriage allows your expectations to take root and grow in the rich soil of a permanent relationship.

RACHEL AND TIM'S STORY

Though Rachel was raised in a supposedly Christian home, she grew up in an atmosphere of abuse. When she left home, she had emotional wounds that she hoped to bandage with a loving relationship. In a desperate search for love, she found herself drawn to a coworker who showed her affection. Her vulnerability was attractive to him, and soon Rachel and Bruce found themselves in a whirlwind romance.

But Rachel's story is complicated: Bruce was married.

Repeating patterns she learned growing up in an emotionally unavailable family, Rachel had fallen in love with a man who could not commit to her. To feel connected to Bruce, Rachel quickly allowed their relationship to become sexual. Whenever she felt their relationship had fallen to second place in Bruce's life, she brought him back into her arms with the allure of sex. But at the end of the day, he always said goodbye and headed home to his family.

During the next few years, Rachel became more desperate for love than ever. She knew in her heart that she wasn't Bruce's priority. Finally she convinced herself that she deserved more. One day at church, she could ignore the conviction in her heart no more. She decided to walk away from Bruce once and for all and to put her future in God's hands. God brought healing and hope into Rachel's life, and five years later, she met and ultimately became engaged to Tim, the man of her dreams.

Rachel and Tim vowed to save their sexual relationship for marriage. Tim, aware of her past, was very sensitive toward Rachel and wanted to do everything he could to cherish and love her. Finally, their wedding night arrived, and they looked forward to sharing complete intimacy with one another. But as the evening progressed, Rachel was haunted by images, emotions, and memories of her past. Flashbacks of her abuse, her relationship with Bruce, and her wounded sexuality brought painful feelings during a time that was supposed to be intimate and sacred. The sexual experiences of her past were seeping into her expectations in the here and now, and she was frightened, anxious, and vulnerable.

Thankfully, Tim's love for Rachel had nothing to do with their sexual relationship and everything to do with her. More than anything, he desired to comfort her and hold her close without the pressure of sex. *She* was his priority, not what she could offer him.

During the following months, God used Tim to give Rachel a glimpse of what it means to be loved unconditionally. She experienced a love that wrapped itself around her and brought the security she had never known. She continued to work toward healing. Though sometimes it was challenging, she had new experiences and formed new expectations with a loving and patient husband. Rachel and Tim have been married for more than fifteen years, and the fruit of their hard work is evident in their relationship.

I last met with Rachel on a Sunday afternoon. She had a smile on her face as she explained that Tim had taken the job of his dreams as the head pastor of a church. Her smile was sly as she told me how fulfilling it is to sit in church listening to her godly pastor-husband speaking to a congregation, thinking about the crazy awesome sex they had the night before and feeling not one hint of guilt or shame. Sex within the context of unconditional committed love is amazing.

It was meant to be. God had restored that to her, and for that she was grateful.

I'm so thankful that we serve a God who doesn't hold our choices and sins against us forever but uses them to teach us and mature us. He restores to us the joys that this life has ravaged (Joel 2:25) if we are willing to change, if we are willing to accept that he knows best.

RESTORING VIRGINITY

No matter how deeply you may have been involved in premarital sex, it is never too late to restore virginity in your life and in the life of your significant other. In addition to the physical exchange in sex, there is an emotional component that is even more meaningful. While you will never be able to change the actions you've chosen in your past, it is never too late to start the process of emotional healing and to seek to make new choices about sex. Restoring virginity has very little to do with the choices you've made in the past and has everything to do with what you are choosing from this day forward. Don't allow guilt and shame to tear your relationship apart, but together choose to give your relationship the honor that it deserves.

Shift Your Thinking

The first step in any kind of change is to shift your beliefs. If you find yourself struggling to give up your nonmarital sexual relationship, I recommend you take some time to really wrestle with your beliefs and deep-seated needs. Purity has less to do with the condition of the body than with the condition of the soul. We should see it not as an obligation but rather as an act of love for and a gesture of trust in a God who knows what makes us tick.

Sometimes we view the pursuit of sex like the child gazing longingly at a cookie jar his evil stepmother told him to stay away from. This perspective can cause us to feel manipulated, cheated, and controlled. Instead, we should see sex as a gift, like an expensive bottle of wine reserved for the perfect time to enjoy. God's role, then, is not that of a cruel dictator but that of a loving Father who wants us to enjoy the very best life has to offer. As Song of Solomon 8:4 charges, "Do not arouse or awaken love until it so desires." Sexual desire can be awakened far too easily, not only robbing you of so many joys but also having devastating effects on your relationship. Consider where your heart is toward God and toward your partner, and commit to storing up your desire for sex until you have entered marriage and may enjoy unrestrained pleasure for a lifetime.

Set Boundaries

Purity doesn't just happen. You can't just wish it into existence, no matter how badly you want it.

When it's cold outside and I am missing the summer months, I sometimes get the strong desire to be in Florida lying out at the beach. I can imagine the sand between my toes, the crashing of the waves, and my husband snoozing beside me, knocked out by the warmth of the sun. I can't even tell you how badly I want to be in Florida sometimes. But wishing to be there, even with all my heart, won't transport me there. I need to get in my car and start driving. And I need to have a plan. If I just chant the word *Florida* all the while I'm driving, and dream of the waves and the sun and the seagulls flying overhead, I could very well end up in Canada, and that would be really bad. (I'm just kidding, my Canadian cousins! Well, sort of.)

It takes time, energy, planning, and commitment to get where you want to go, particularly in the area of sexual boundaries, and especially for those who have traveled down the sexual path before. You need to set boundaries that will keep you from awakening the desires that you are hoping to reserve.

Before I list some examples, let me say that boundaries alone will not get you anywhere. They are just one piece of the puzzle, a way to control your body as you wait on God's plan for your sex life.

Here are some examples of healthy boundaries:

- Don't allow physical contact below the neck.
- Don't lay down together (couch, bed, floor).
- Avoid kissing after a set time (e.g., 9:00 p.m.).
- Refrain from sexually stimulating conversation and sexual references.
- Spend more time (or all of your time) in public places.
- Always keep your clothes on.
- Say no to sexually stimulating situations (watching certain movies, going to certain places).
- And my favorite extra tip for the ladies: don't shave your legs!

Find Alternatives

According to Rob Bell's insightful book *Sex God*,[8] human beings are drawn to sex because we were created to connect with others, and sex is a connector. I love this idea because it acknowledges and normalizes an important human desire rather than using it to cause shame. We were made to connect because we were made to be in relationship with the God who designed us for himself, the God who longs to be in relationship with us.

Since the desire for sex and ultimately connection is so natural and so good, it's important not to repress it but rather to use it in a beneficial way. Bell suggests that we channel our sexual desires into doing something beneficial for others. We sometimes talk of channeling anger or passion or power into doing something useful, rather than doing something negative. How profound to think of channeling our sexuality in the same way.

When I work with men and women who want to change in some way (lose weight, kick a drug or alcohol habit, get control of time or finances), I always emphasize channeling their desires into new behaviors. It's one thing to shift your thinking and to create boundaries, but ultimately these are only the first steps. For true change and development to occur, you must find substitutes for negative behaviors. "I used to do that; now I do this instead." Removing a behavior from your life leaves a gaping hole. If that hole is not filled, the negative behavior will find its way back into your life. And sometimes it will settle in more deeply and become stronger than it was before.

> **FAQ 18**
> I know going all the way can be damaging to a relationship, but how far is too far?

You must find something to fill the gap. What are you passionate about? Where do you feel the most connected? What gives you purpose and makes you feel significant? Invest in those things. Find community. Seek deeper friendships. Give of your time and talents. Pursue your dreams. Have conversations. Invest in yourself. Do whatever you can to find that connection with both God and the world around you, to channel your sexuality in a healthy and holy way.

If these questions are hard for you to answer and you don't quite know where your passions lie, then it's important to return to dating inward to get to know yourself, because therein lies the answer to mastering the struggles that come with dating outward.

Seek Accountability

Whether you are restoring or maintaining your desire to wait for sex, you can't do it alone, though it's tempting to try. Some people want to rely on the person with whom they are having sexual interaction for help. Honestly, that's about as effective as asking a person stuck in a pit with you to get you out. Sometimes help can come only when you are willing to look up and call out.

Particularly for those who are in a serious dating relationship or for those who have a sexual history, it's important to invite someone into your struggles. No one *wants* to share their sexual struggles with someone else. And that's precisely what makes accountability such an important component of restoring and maintaining virginity.

Seek a mentor, friend, pastor, or family member who will love and support you, someone who is willing to get involved and help you make things right. List the reasons you are waiting for sex as well as the sexual behaviors that you are caught up in. Share your list with a trusted person who is willing to hold you to your commitment by asking the hard questions and being willing to listen to whatever you need to confide.

Believe it or not, the accountability relationship that brought me the most healing was with one of my college professors. She encouraged me, directed me, and, most important, loved me through some of the hardest places in my life. She never pointed a finger at me or looked down on me because of my sins, but rather connected with me through her past struggles, and then used that connection to lift me to higher places. She always accepted me where I was but never let me stay there.

The goal of accountability is not shame but restoration. Find someone who believes in that to walk by your side and keep you on track.

The season before marriage is meant to be a time of great awareness, a time of preparing for one of the most incredible yet complex journeys you will ever take. Don't allow the physical connection that is intended to bring you together as one to be the very thing that tears you apart. Treat your sexuality as the precious gift that God means for it to be.

Questions for Reflection

1. What influences have shaped your views on sex?

2. In what ways has your sexual past had an impact on your life?

3. Have you taken a passive or an active role in reserving sexual intimacy for marriage? What steps are you willing to take to restore your virginity?

4. What can you do to channel your sexuality to connect with others in a healthy way?

PART THREE

DATING UPWARD

THE TRIANGLE THEORY
Me, You, and Jesus?

"$a^2 + b^2 = c^2$"

I'll never forget the details of our wedding day. It truly was perfect in every way, and my husband and I love to reminisce about everything from the ceremony to the reception and beyond.

One thing that both of us will always remember is the sermon our pastor gave during the ceremony. Right before we said our vows, our pastor pulled out of his pocket a few shapes that he had borrowed from the church nursery. Nursery toys? John and I gave each other a nervous glance, not knowing where Pastor Rob was going with this.

In his sermon, Pastor Rob talked about how each of the basic shapes can be given a profound meaning for marriage, and said that if we remembered the principles associated with them, our marriage would thrive. When he got to the triangle, he explained that our marriage is a trinity because of the importance of our individual relationships with God within our marriage. If we included God in our marriage, he would be the spiritual and emotional glue that would hold us together.

I remember a talk I attended at a conference in my late teens in which the speaker explained our relationships with God and our significant other in similar terms. He drew a triangle on the board and labeled the top point God. He then labeled the bottom two corners You and Significant Other. He then explained that we are each on a spiritual journey, a journey that ultimately we make alone. But the closer we each get to God, the closer we come to each other.

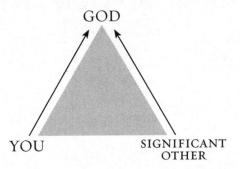

I see this concept at work every day in my relationship with my husband. In our individual lives, as we draw nearer to God, our emotional ties run deeper, our spiritual bond holds stronger, and our physical connection becomes more vibrant.

But drawing closer to God isn't some magical process. It has nothing to do with church attendance, minutes logged in daily devotions, or how many people we have on our prayer list. Our spiritual journey is about the transformational work of Jesus Christ in our lives. The more time we spend in God's presence, the more we are transformed into the image of his Son. And the more we reflect Jesus' character in our lives, the more magnetic we become to one another. We are drawn together by a love that is beyond our limited capacity, the limitless love of God that pours into us and overflows into the life of the other.

THE DATING TRIANGLE

I really appreciate the triangle imagery, because for the longest time as a single woman (and long before I met John) that's how I imagined my spiritual journey. I wanted to live in a way that would bring me to meet the man of my dreams. I believed that the closer I became to

God, the more I would be aligned with his will and, hopefully, with the person I would someday marry.

Yet though I had that hope in my heart, I found myself living out an entirely different theory in my life. I got distracted and put all my energy into horizontal relationships with possible boyfriends or mates, investing very little in my relationship with God. I was preoccupied with finding my soul mate. I attended ministry events and church meetings and did a lot of volunteering. These things were all great in and of themselves, but I was doing them for the wrong reasons. I was driven by my need to connect horizontally, rather than to connect vertically. Simply put, I was hunting for a man.

My thinking was distorted. I was trying to get to a spouse *by way* of my relationship with God. I was taking advantage of God, in a sense, trying to get closer to him by doing things for him in order to receive the blessing of a spouse, rather than because I wanted to serve him and to love him.

It wasn't until my junior year of college that I finally acted on the belief that if Jesus was my priority, I wouldn't have to worry about anything else. If I

> **FAQ 19**
> I am dating a Christian, but our spirituality never seems to come up. What do I do?

made him the center of my life and pursued him the best I knew how, he would take care of the details. The apostle Matthew puts it this way: "What I'm trying to do here is to get you to relax, to not be so preoccupied with *getting*, so you can respond to God's *giving*. People who don't know God and the way he works fuss over these things, but you know both God and how he works. Steep your life in God-reality, God-initiative, God-provisions. Don't worry about missing out. You'll find all your everyday human concerns will be met" (Matt. 6:31 – 33 MSG).

I decided to stop taking the horizontal approach to dating and began to focus vertically. I lifted my eyes upward, in pursuit of my relationship with Jesus. From the outside, my life didn't change that much. I was involved in the same things and spent time with the same people. But, oh, did my heart change. Rather than carrying my mental checklist around all the time as I looked for a spouse, I fixed my heart on finding Jesus in the routine of my day. I sought to connect with him, to interact with him, and to focus my heart on what I could give rather than on what I could receive. It took a lot of practice to keep my mind occupied with Jesus. But with each day that passed I found my heart fixed more on heaven and fixed less on the things of earth.

When your heart is focused on the eternal, the temporal world takes on new shape and meaning. It loses power in your life, freeing you to live fully. Your relationship status and your desire to be married may never disappear, but they stop controlling your life. And you can trust in God's promise that "you'll find all your everyday human concerns will be met."

A MAN WITH AN UPWARD FOCUS

They predicted that he would be the last one of his friends to be married. Even though he was good looking, could slam dunk a basketball, and had a natural year-round tan, his friends just didn't grasp how he would ever find a wife with his seemingly passive approach. Friday nights were the prime time to cruise the city, catch a drink, and scope out the dating scene, trying to hook a mate, but he found himself uninterested in this approach.

It wasn't that girls didn't interest him; it was that his heart longed for more than just that. He wanted to see the bigger story, the journey that God had mapped for his life. He hoped that marriage and a family would one day be a part of that, but he knew that he would have to leave that up to God. He knew that when he fixed his eyes on Jesus, everything else would fall into place.

He practiced this belief by living his life upward. While all of his friends chose to connect with the opposite sex as often as possible, he chose to connect with God, to seek his kingdom first. When his friends were out partying on Friday nights, he stayed in his dorm room reading up on apologetics, listening to challenging sermons, and trying to become the man God wanted him to be.

And I'm so glad he did, because on July 2, 2005, my world collided with this six-foot-four stud. I noticed him immediately in the group of young adults at the confer-

> **FAQ 20**
> Is it okay for a Christian to date a non-Christian?

ence that day. It's amazing when you can see someone's heart just as clearly as you can see their face. His upward focus was so obvious in the way he interacted with the world around him. The fruit of God's Spirit was overflowing from his life (Gal. 5:22 – 23). It drew me to him. But the most beautiful part of this story is that it is John's upward focus that is still drawing me to his side every single day.

ANDERSON AND TAJ'S STORY

It took a huge leap of faith for a country boy like Anderson to sign up for a trip halfway across the world. He was used to the comfort of his family, friends, and the simple life. But as his relationship with God grew stronger, he no longer could ignore the desire in his heart to go. God was calling him out of his comfort zone and into some of the most impoverished areas in the world.

Upon arriving in the Philippines, Anderson realized that there would be a lot to grow accustomed to. The food, the heat, the smells, and the language all were a shock to his system. But soon he grew to love the Filipino people, and God used his desire to serve and bless them in mutually significant ways.

The most significant thing he remembers about this trip is that it really brought him to a complete dependence on the Lord. Having no friends and family to rely on in unfamiliar surroundings, he was able to get through his days only by drawing on God's strength.

His deepening relationship with God provided him with blessings beyond anything he'd ever received before. And just when he thought he couldn't be any more blessed, he found himself working side by side with a woman he soon fell in love with.

> **FAQ 21**
> What about "missionary dating"?

Taj, a native of the Philippines, was surprised to find an American boy serving alongside her, especially in that part of town. Each day, they headed to some of the most impoverished parts of the city and passed out food to the hungry. As they served God together, a strong friendship developed. As the time approached for Anderson to leave the Philippines, they decided to keep in contact.

Though they kept their feelings to themselves, the Lord was planting seeds in their hearts. A few months later, Anderson was back in the Philippines, this time pursuing the heart of a woman he had never imagined he would fall in love with. God blessed their upward focus, and they were engaged and then married shortly after.

I love being around Anderson and Taj. Their love for each other is so deep that you can feel it just by being around them. The way they look at each other, talk to each other, and treat each other are sure signs of the romance God has blessed them with. But more than anything, I love being around them because they exude their love for God. It's almost as though you can see the very fibers of their relationship with God just binding them together. They are so in love with each other, but they are in love with him first.

DATING UPWARD

It's always encouraging to hear stories like Anderson and Taj's. Who doesn't love to hear about that kind of a romance? But more than just being encouraged by such stories, it's important to create your own.

I remember when I was just learning to drive. I tended to look at the part of the road right before my front bumper. I felt a lot of pressure, and I wanted to make sure I was staying between those darned yellow lines. My license and freedom depended on it! But the more I looked down at the road in front of me, the more I lost track of the curves and turns ahead. My dad constantly had to remind me to shift my focus upward to look at what was ahead.

It's time to get real with yourself and assess where your eyes are focused. What road are you headed down, and what direction is it taking you? As C. S. Lewis so eloquently writes, "Aim at heaven, and you will get earth thrown in. Aim at earth, and you will get neither." So ask yourself whether your steps are guided by the goal of connecting with God. Or are you pursuing other things? Do you believe that the best way to find true love is to align your journey with him? Do you agree that he knows what is best for you, or rather who is best for you? Is your aim toward heaven, or is it stuck here on earth?

Is your focus outward or upward?

Questions for Reflection

1. Are you preoccupied with horizontal relationships or with your vertical relationship with God?
2. What role does God play in your life?
3. Look up the following verses: 2 Chronicles 20:12; Psalm 141:8; Psalm 25:15; 2 Corinthians 4:18; Hebrews 12:2; Philippians 3:14. What is the overall theme of these verses? Can you find other verses that also focus on this idea?
4. List some practical steps you can take to bring your focus upward.

CHAPTER 10

WHAT RELATIONSHIPS CAN'T DO
The Cup Analogy

"I feel like I'm whole again!"

The contrast between the woman I was speaking to now and the woman I had spoken to only a few short weeks ago was astonishing. Angela had come for counseling a few months back hoping to sort through some things in her life. Having lived through a serious car accident, and battling some major stressors in her life, at times she found herself with little motivation to go on. Before all these things had happened, she had so many dreams of where she would be in her late twenties. Single, broke, and living with her parents was not what she expected. She was depressed and needed support and guidance.

Therapy started off great. We quickly got to the root of some of her struggles and set some attainable goals for therapy. She felt encouraged and began to take steps to grow and find her purpose again. But suddenly, something changed. One day Angela came into therapy announcing that she felt healed. All better. No problems. Just like that.

The answer? Angela had met a guy. "I met him last week, and he is everything I ever could have dreamed of. He's funny, charming, and totally handsome. He owns his own house, drives an awesome car, and is a really hard worker. He wants to love me, support me, and help me get on my feet. I'm so excited! I feel like I'm whole again!"

My stomach sank when I heard those words. Here was a perfectly capable, beautiful, talented young woman who believed that all of her problems would dissolve in the arms of a man.

IS YOUR CUP FULL?

"Is the cup half empty, or half full?"

According to popular psychology, the answer to this question reveals whether a person is an optimist or a pessimist. Those who see the cup as half empty tend to look on the negative side of life, while those who see it as half full live on the bright side.

Using the cup as a metaphor, it's important to recognize that throughout our lives, our emotional cups fluctuate between being empty and being full. When I meet with clients, I am less concerned with whether they see the cup as half empty or half full. Instead, I find myself asking them to consider how full they feel.

One thing I've observed when working with young adults like Angela is that some of them tend to live their lives at the half-full mark. Feelings of inadequacy, insecurities, and a lack of self-worth prevent them from living the full lives that God has created for them. Because they don't deal with these negative feelings, their emotional cups keep draining, one drop at a time. They feel empty and deficient, and ultimately seek out relationships in the hope of being filled. They bring their wounds to relationships for bandaging, not realizing that two broken people can never be the source of healing for one another.

Ironically, it is those who enter relationships feeling incomplete who wind up in the most dysfunctional relationships, because there is a correlation between your level of fulfillment and your ability to connect with others in a healthy way. Relationships can never make you whole, because they never were intended to. Some of the most devastating relationships I've seen are between people who place that unrealistic expectation on one another. You will never feel whole in the presence of your mate if you don't feel whole standing alone. You will never feel loved in the arms of your spouse if you haven't first learned to love yourself. You will never be able to give to your partner if you have never learned to get your needs met. Healthy relationships are meaningful, not magical.

There is no denying that the pursuit of a relationship can be a positive thing. Marriage is a great blessing, and anyone who finds a good spouse has found a great gift (Prov. 18:22). I can wholeheartedly say that my marriage has enriched my life in so many ways. It has been a source of great joy and encouragement. It has sharpened me and pushed me to become a better person. It has poured many blessings into my emotional cup. Yet for all the things that marriage has done to enhance my life and stretch my love, there are still some things that it will never be able to do.

WHAT RELATIONSHIPS CAN'T DO
Relationships Can't Erase Your Insecurities

It might sound like being loved unconditionally by another human would help us to feel better about ourselves, that being married and being loved by another would teach us how to love ourselves. But that way of thinking has done more harm than good. Putting such expectations on a person will only cause damage, because no one can change how we view ourselves. No one has the power to deal with our inadequacies and insecurities but ourselves.

No matter how much encouragement, affection, affirmation, and validation you receive from your partner, security comes when you choose to see yourself through the eyes of God, not through the eyes of your significant other. No human being can offer you what is needed for true value and self-worth. True security comes only within the framework of your relationship with God.

Relationships Can't Give You Purpose

One thing I noticed while attending college was many of my peers' all-consuming search for a spouse. Don't get me wrong, I was on the lookout too. But something behind this drive really disturbed me. Their sole purpose in life was to catch a mate.

> **FAQ 22**
> How do I deal with insecurities in a relationship?

Something has gone terribly wrong when young Christians believe that their main purpose in life is to find marital love. This dangerous belief robs us of joy and true purpose. True purpose is eternal, because God's plan for our lives can never be taken away. The Bible encourages us to live for God's glory, to love him and to love others in an attempt to leave his fingerprints all across this world (Matt. 22:36 – 40). We are each made for a purpose that, while it may include marriage, is much larger than marriage. Though marriage can be an incredible gift, it is a means to an end, not the end itself.

When we see marriage as our sole purpose, we find ourselves with nowhere to go when we finally arrive. Marriage may be an avenue in fulfilling our purpose, but it's not the destination. There is so much life to be lived before marriage, through marriage, and even beyond marriage. We need to seek God's purpose for our lives beyond finding a spouse, allowing his will and his plan to guide us. Rather than asking what God can do for us, we need to ask what we can do for him. In this is true purpose. And you just might run into a spouse along the way.

Relationships Can't Bring You Healing

I was doing some house cleaning the other day when my toddler, Ella, decided to join me. Without my knowledge, she grabbed the dirty washcloth that I had been using to scrub and disinfect and went to town "wiping down" all our clean furniture. Needless to say, the furniture was no longer clean after that. Despite Ella's good intentions, the dirty washcloth she used couldn't clean effectively.

Similar to the way Ella couldn't get the furniture clean with a dirty washcloth, we can't bring complete emotional healing into the life of another person, because we are also wounded, sinful, and flawed. Even with our best intentions, we are ineffective in the end.

Marriage is about finding a comrade, not ultimate contentment. It's about finding a helpmate, not a healer (Gen. 2:18). You must see the road to healing as a journey with God, one that you and he must walk together.

WHAT JESUS DOES

The Bible explains that because of sin, we are born into this world broken, helpless, and lost. Add to that the struggles and wounds we experience in life, and we are guaranteed to be lacking, empty, and incomplete, desperately in need of a Savior.

Though our salvation can never come from an earthly relationship, there is one relationship that can bring healing. According to Scripture, our relationship with God through Jesus Christ is the path to a healing that

> **FAQ 23**
> Should you ever date someone you wouldn't consider marrying?

knows no bounds. Through Jesus, we can be delivered from the emotional wounds of our past, the mistakes and choices of our present, and the eternal pain of our future.

"'He himself bore our sins' in his body on the cross, so that we might die to sins and live for righteousness; 'by his wounds you have been healed'" (1 Peter 2:24).

Friends, there is so much freedom in grasping what Jesus did for you. He has provided the opportunity for you to be healed and whole. Unlike so many relationships here on earth, this healing relationship is always available, waiting for you to believe and accept. Being in relationship with Jesus allows him to take your wounds upon himself. You are given the opportunity to exchange your brokenness for completeness, your deficits and insecurities for his strength (2 Cor. 12:9). Something supernatural happens when you enter into relationship with Jesus. As a mark of your intimate relationship with God, he places his Spirit inside of you (1 Cor. 3:16). By the power of his Spirit, you are enabled to live and to move and to be (Acts 17:28). You are ushered from your old self into something new (2 Cor. 5:17). Your emotional cup can finally be full, even to the point of overflowing.

My husband will always carry a vivid picture of this concept in his mind. When he was younger, his dad brought him and his brothers to the kitchen table. He began pouring milk into the empty glass that was sitting in front of them. Eventually, the glass got so full that the milk began to spill out onto the table. He lovingly explained to his three boys that whatever is in your heart eventually will make its way out. When God's presence, love, and power are poured into your life, they inevitably overflow into the lives of those around you.

"You anoint my head with oil; my cup overflows" (Ps. 23:5).

There is something magical about a relationship that is birthed out of the overflow of the heart. In this kind of relationship, two people are giving to each other out of their fullness, rather than taking from each other out of their emptiness.

The possibility of this kind of relationship may sound wonderful but too good to be true. In a world littered with brokenness, sin, and selfishness, is it even possible to achieve "fullness in Jesus"? I, too, wrestle with this question. Though I am constantly striving to be made complete through my relationship with God, the truth of the matter is that there are still days when I find myself bogged down in the world around me. There are times when I give in to the temptation to find my value in things other than my relationship with Jesus.

Yet through my victories and my failures, I have come to terms with the truth that I am a work in progress. And so are you.

So where do we go from here?

WHAT YOU CAN DO

There are works in progress all around us, though we don't always recognize them. An artist facing a blank canvas, slowly painting each brushstroke, is in fact a work in progress. A college student taking an exam, hoping to achieve one more grade toward his degree, is a work in progress. A woman carrying a baby within her womb, counting down the weeks until she meets her child, is a work in progress. Everything, from nature to technology, is part of the process of becoming. Becoming better, smarter, healthier. And even becoming complete.

Even our relationship with God is a process. Recognizing that it is only in relationship with God that we can achieve fullness, let's take a look at our role in this special relationship.

Scripture deliberately uses relationship terms to describe our interactions with God. We are called sons, friends, and children of God (Gal. 4:7; John 15:15; Gal. 3:26). We are even called his bride (Rev. 19:7). These are terms of relational intimacy, reminding us that we are participants in this relationship. We are called both to receive and to reciprocate love. The most important thing we can do in fostering our relationship with God is to love him back.

As we learn to love God, it's crucial to remember that love is more than a feeling. It's a choice. Because we can't always trust our feelings, we display our commitment to love most clearly in the choices we make every day.

For me, fostering my relationship with God has involved spiritual practices that remind me of my relationship with him. I've felt most connected to God through reading his Word, interacting with him through prayer, and being vulnerable before him through worship. I've learned to love God by being surrounded by men and women who also love him. I've come to adore his heart by serving others the way that Jesus did. Through loving him and allowing him to love me, I've become fuller and more complete.

But I'm also a work in progress. This world and the people in it deplete me of my energy, my strength, and my value each and every day. Loving God is a continual process, one that I must engage in each day to become full again — and again and again.

My challenge for you is to take a look at your life and evaluate the condition of your emotional cup. Consider how much you have allowed Jesus to bring security, purpose, and healing into your life here and now. Rather than seeing the pursuit of true love as the piece missing from your puzzle, consider that the missing piece is the only Love that truly completes.

Questions for Reflection

1. How full is your emotional cup?
2. What things do you tend to rely on to complete you and fill you up?
3. Have you used relationships as a means of feeling filled and valued? What has been the result?
4. Are you willing to take the steps of believing what Jesus has done, accepting his love for you, and reciprocating his love?

CHAPTER 11

HOW TO DATE
WITH NO REGRETS

"I really want to kiss you right now."

There is probably no other phrase that can get a heart to flutter more. To some, a kiss is just a kiss, but in reality it's so much more. Being so closely connected to someone through the touching of lips — it's a moment of vulnerability, of intimacy, of trust. It's the moment when two hearts connect through the avenue of the physical.

"But I don't think it's a good idea," he went on to say.

It was late November. The beauty of fall had dissolved into the cold dark evenings of winter. John and I were hanging out at his apartment on a Sunday afternoon, watching a football game. It was about five months after we had met, and our friendship was budding into a dating relationship.

I can't tell you what game was on or who won, because the entire two hours, I was trying to figure out what to do with the strong feelings that I had for him. I was falling for him hard, and everything within me was hoping he would just lean over and give me a kiss. Some sort of sign that we were on the same page. The funny thing is that I thought I was acting pretty nonchalant. It's not like I was staring into his eyes with my lips puckered. But somehow he saw right through me. The other day, while we were reminiscing about that moment, he told me that my eyes had said it all; it had been obvious that I wanted him to kiss me.

His response? Not yet.

I was floored. In my experience, it was rare to meet a young man who would turn down a kiss. Don't get me wrong, I know of some people who saved their first kiss for marriage. I respect and admire their self-control. But it wasn't something I was accustomed to.

So what does a kiss have to do with dating with no regrets? Everything.

One of the hardest things about dating is learning to live beyond the moment. Caught up in the whirlwind of passion, it's so easy to choose what feels good without considering how that choice will affect the future. It's easy to live for the moment, isn't it? Choosing to eat that chocolate bar staring at you from the vending machine when you're trying to kick extra calories. Choosing to watch that movie on TV that caught your attention when you should be studying for your chemistry test. Living for the here and now might not cause major damage every time, but choosing immediate gratification in your dating relationships is a recipe for regret.

I learned a lot about dating upward from John. Looking back on my dating history, I definitely have regrets, but he can honestly tell you that he doesn't have many. You see, his goal never was simply to snag a date; it was to honor God and draw closer to him throughout all of his interactions with me. He was willing to say no to what he wanted for the sake of what was holy.

HOLY EATING, HOLY DRINKING

One of the biggest mistakes Christians make is to believe that holiness has anything to do with religiousness. When we think of becoming more like Jesus, our minds go immediately to "the spiritual." I find myself getting caught in this trap too, believing that becoming more like Jesus means more prayer, more church services, and more ministry activity.

Though we do come to understand Jesus' heart through such activities, I think we miss much of what it means to become like Jesus when we fail to honor him through ordinary, day-to-day things. Like it or not, if we compartmentalize our lives into "spiritual" and "nonspiritual" activities, a huge percentage will fall into the latter category. Our lives are made up of mundane activities like eating and drinking and sleeping.

But this is the beauty of living a life with no regrets: it is in the ordinary that we can most see God as extraordinary. The Bible puts it this way: "So whether you eat or drink or whatever you do, do it all for the glory of God" (1 Cor. 10:31). Becoming like Jesus has little to do with *what* you are doing, and everything to do with *how* you are doing it.

We are asked to glorify God in all we do, so what does that mean in dating?

HOLY DATING

My dating relationship with John is a great example of what it means to date with no regrets. As I look through my journals, I see so much evidence of our deliberately pursuing holiness during our friendship and into our dating relationship. Throughout our relationship, my heart's desire was to fix my eyes on Jesus and to let him lead the way. When my heart's desire was to fall more in love with Jesus, the finish line was easier to reach because it had little to do with marriage and everything to do with drawing closer to him.

My journal entry found me thinking through some of these things:

> I'm very excited to see what's to come ... I'm looking forward to the day when we'll be able to reveal what's in our hearts to one another.

I'm thankful that John is a man of God who is seeking the will of God over his own will. I'm thankful for his respect, maturity, and wisdom.

At the same time, there is no trusting anything but the Lord's leading. Right now, that is my goal. Wait and pray.

"Almighty God, you alone can bring into order the unruly wills and affections of sinners. Grant your people grace to love what you command and desire what you promise; that, among the swift and varied changes of the world, our hearts may surely be fixed where true joys are to be found" (*Passion and Purity*).

When our hearts are fixed where true joys are found, we will experience no regrets in our season of dating, only lessons learned. When our eyes are set on Jesus, the change that takes place in our hearts has eternal significance. "So we fix our eyes not on what is seen, but on what is unseen, since what is seen is temporary, but what is unseen is eternal" (2 Cor. 4:18).

EYES ON HIM (WITH A CAPITAL H)

For many young adults, the college years have a ripple effect through the rest of their lives. The classes they take open doors to interests and passions that usher them into careers. The friends they make shape who they will become. The people they date have a special connection to their hearts, adding to them or taking away from them.

I enjoyed the freedom I experienced in my college years, but at the same time I was aware that every step I took would affect my future, and I felt a great sense of responsibility.

During my junior year of college, this was especially true. It was a season of new beginnings. The semester before, I had decided to break up with my boyfriend of one and a half years. The breakup had brought a wave of anxiety. I felt lost in the transition and wasn't sure where I fit anymore. But in my confusion, God placed me in a dorm that had a significant impact on my focus.

I met Sarah in my sophomore year of college. It's no exaggeration to say that she seemed to be the most likeable person on campus, and lucky for me, we also happened to be dorm-mates. I didn't know at the time that she would become a lifelong friend and that our friendship would impact the way I view relationships.

For Sarah, falling in love and meeting a husband was never a priority. She lived a life that placed God at the center of her attention. More than anything, she was out to connect with God and reach out to others. And she did that so well.

After my difficult breakup, Sarah shared with me a passage from the Bible. God's people were about to be attacked by their enemy. They were outnumbered and afraid and had no idea what to do. And in their confusion, they faithfully cried out to God, "We do not know what to do, but our eyes are on you" (2 Chron. 20:12). Despite what was going on around them, they were able to fix their eyes upward and trust God to bring them through. That seemed to be the theme of Sarah's life. And that year, it was a theme that shaped my perspective and began to take root in my heart as I learned to close my eyes to my past and instead open them to what God was doing.

The world of dating may not be a literal battle, but there is definitely a war taking place. We are in a spiritual war with an enemy who wants to rob us of hope and joy and fill us with shame and regret. Satan hates healthy relationships, because he despises everything that is from the hand of God. He wants to destroy our relationship with God and to sabotage our marriages long before they even begin. The best way he can do that is by getting us to take our focus off of the one who invented relationships and place it on everything else.

In your season of dating, fix your eyes on Jesus. Don't become so consumed by your pursuit of the opposite sex that it becomes your idol, prioritized above all else. Dating with no regrets means keeping your focus on Jesus, so that no matter what happens in your relationships with others, your relationship with God remains intact.

REMAIN YOU

We all have had that friend who suddenly disappeared from the face of the earth. One day we were enjoying their company, hanging out, going to movies, going out to dinner, and spending time together. And the next, they were missing in action. Nowhere to be found. Swallowed up by the abyss of a new romantic relationship. No more time for friends, hobbies, or fun. All of a sudden their lives revolved around their new love interest, and everything else lost its significance.

Nine months later: ugly breakup. Our friend comes back on the scene, hoping to reconnect and put the pieces of her life back together. But she is no longer herself. Having exchanged who she was for her relationship, she has to find herself all over again. Fooled into building her life on a romance, she had put everything and everyone else aside. And now that the ground beneath her has crumbled, she has to rebuild.

To date with no regrets, don't build your house on the sand of a dating relationship (Matt. 7:26 – 27). Don't invest your entire life in someone else, forsaking who you are.

KRISTY'S STORY

Everyone expected Kristy to do great things. She was a high school senior and a straight-A student with lots of friends. With a music scholarship lined up at the college of her dreams, she had big plans. But all that changed the moment she met Barry. They met at a party and were instantly attracted to each other. Barry was a few years older than her, and she found herself drawn to the man in him. He wasn't much for books and had dropped out of high school to make a living. In her eyes, he was a responsible man, different from all the seniors she knew.

They started dating, and soon their relationship became all consuming. Outside of school, Kristy spent every waking moment with

Barry. He would pick her up after work, and she would spend the evening with him, forsaking her friends, her family, and her schoolwork. Her friendships dissolved, her grades suffered, and her passion for music went by the wayside. On top of it all, within just a few months, Kristy and Barry made plans to move in together. Soon her relationship with her family was so strained that she felt that all she had left was Barry.

> ### FAQ 24
> How do I deal with the pain of a breakup?

Blinded by her romance, Kristy forgot who she was and where she came from. She lost sight of her goals and dreams, and invested everything she had in Barry. His life became hers.

I met Kristy two years after her breakup. She was living with a female coworker, trying to restore her relationships with her family and friends. She had lost her scholarship after her grades plummeted, and was working full time at an ice cream shop while studying for her GED. Her relationship with Barry had devastated her life. She had exchanged her future for the unreliable promise of a dating relationship, and now was trying to salvage what she could.

Maybe you have made similar mistakes. Maybe you've found yourself living with regrets. Caught up in a short-term view of relationships, you've lost sight of your life, your future, and the world around you.

No-regrets dating means that you keep yourself intact during your pursuit of true love by remaining faithful to God, to yourself, and to the life that you've been called to. Be wise with your energy and your time, giving only some to your significant other rather than allowing him or her to consume it all. Remain yourself, and trust that true love will find you just as you are.

• • •

I knew John was the right man for me because he so easily fit into my life, and I into his. Though we were drawing closer to each other through our dating relationship, I was free to remain myself. I was able to focus on the people and things that mattered to me, and was never asked to exchange who I was for a relationship with him. I continued to invest in my friendships, remaining close to my family, working toward my goals and dreams, and drawing closer to God. In fact, my relationship with John pushed me toward these things and challenged me to be true to myself rather than being true only to my relationship with him. At the end of our season of dating, not only were we standing at the altar together, but we also had no regrets.

Questions for Reflection

1. Looking back on your dating relationships, do you have regrets?

2. If so, what are you doing to work through them and to protect yourself from future regrets?

3. Have you allowed yourself to remain intact throughout your dating relationships? If not, what parts of you have been compromised? How has this impacted your life?

4. How has your relationship with God fared during your dating relationships? What can you do to prioritize your relationship with him?

CHAPTER 12

ALONE NO MORE
Make Room at Your Table for One

"Table for one."

There's a good chance that when you picked up this book, you were sitting alone at a table for one, trying to make sense of the world of singleness. You may have even picked up this book hoping that it would lead you into the arms of your soul mate before the final page, with a money back guarantee. And maybe here you are at the last chapter — no soul mate, no money back, and not even a single date. Sometimes it's really hard to be alone. I would venture to say that loneliness is the hardest part of being single.

THE "GIFT" OF SINGLENESS?

If you come from a Christian circle, there's a good chance you've heard of "the gift of singleness." It's a phrase that is used (and misused) to try to ease the isolation that many young men and women feel during their single years. It's as though singleness is viewed as this extra-special gift, handed out only to those who are strong enough to handle it.

But if singleness is such a gift, then why are so many people refusing to accept it? Why are so many young men and women terrified of being alone? One young woman put it this way: "If singleness is a gift, then I'm keeping the receipt, because I'm planning on returning it!"

She's not alone. I receive hundreds of emails and messages saying the same thing. I could just feel the raw emotion of one young man who wrote, "I'm done with being alone. How can I trust that God will do what's best for my life? How can he create the world in seven days and then it take him nineteen years and counting to help me meet a girl that I'm infatuated with that loves me too? It doesn't make any sense."

If singleness is a gift, then why do so many young men and women feel isolated, desperate, and alone?

OUR DEEPEST NEEDS

I remember a time when I felt utterly alone.

It was my first year of graduate school, and I was living off campus in my own apartment. I was no longer surrounded by the hustle and bustle of college life. Though I had three roommates, we each were wrapped up in doing our own things, and we crossed paths only every now and again.

There were many mornings when I woke up to an empty house, hearing only the quiet tick-tocking of my clock on the wall and the chirping of birds outside my window.

Who knew I was awake? Who even cared? There was no one to reflect with, no one to connect to. No one to witness my life and remind me that it mattered. And in that loneliness, sometimes it felt as though maybe my life *didn't* matter.

There is an underlying, unspoken idea in our Western culture that being alone makes you less of a person somehow, that somehow it takes your value away. Try going to a movie by yourself, or getting a bite to eat alone. Deep down, we fear what people will think. Deep down, being alone makes us feel less.

When it came to longing for marriage, there are so many things it wasn't about for me. It wasn't about the sex. I had held off on that for years; what was just a few more? It wasn't about having someone to take care of me. I was working and in graduate school, paying my bills and managing my money. I was doing a pretty good job of taking care of myself. It wasn't about wanting a family. I was immersed in my inner city ministry, surrounded by children who called me their mom.

No, my desire for marriage had nothing to do with sex or money or family; it had everything to do with not wanting to be alone. I longed for that person to connect with in the early moments of my morning when I opened my eyes (those seemed to be the hardest for me). I wanted someone to share with about my day, my struggles, my plans. I was longing for connection, for companionship, and for comradery.

This is what makes us human. This is what keeps us alive.

So what if our deepest needs are meant not to destroy us but to bring us life? What if our fear of isolation is not the result of something gone wrong but rather a movement toward what is right?

JESUS CAN'T BE YOUR BOYFRIEND

I used to feel so guilty when I was single. I felt guilty for longing for a husband and for not letting Jesus fill the void in my heart. I felt guilty that Jesus was not enough for me, because deep down I longed to be in a relationship, to find true love, to hurry up and get married. As much as I loved Jesus with all of my heart, there still seemed to be room for someone else, a place in my heart that had not yet been filled. Jesus was my Savior, my Redeemer, and my Love, but I never was able to make him my boyfriend.

But there's something I've discovered about this dilemma that I wish someone had told me when I was single: Jesus can't be your boyfriend or girlfriend. I know that's probably not what you were expecting to hear. Trust me, I've been around the block when it comes to reading dating books. They always seem to conclude with a statement that appears to dismiss our struggles and fears and leaves us feeling far more invalidated and frustrated than encouraged: "During this time of singleness, let Jesus be your significant other." Really? Talk about easier said than done, if it can be done at all. In my opinion, that phrase has done far more harm than good.

I think Christians are too hard on themselves. We place expectations on our shoulders that are not only unrealistic but inhuman. Take heart; even God is on your side on this one! God himself saw that it is not good for us to be alone (Gen. 2:18), so he fashioned for Adam a wife. The desire to be intimately connected with another human being has been part of human nature since the beginning of time.

Your longing for an intimate relationship with another person is something you were created to feel. It doesn't mean that you are unholy or that you haven't let Jesus fill your heart the way he should. It means you're human, created in the image of God, a God who loves, who connects, and who longs for relationship himself.

Jesus can never be your boyfriend or girlfriend because he was never intended to be. A significant part of your heart was designed specifically for just him, but there is a part of your heart that was designed specifically for others.

Jesus can never be your boyfriend or girlfriend because he was intended to be so much more than that. He was intended to be your Master, your Savior, and your Healer. He was intended to be your Counselor, your Peace, and the Love of your life. He longs for you to be in relationship with him, but God has made you also to be in relationship with others, because he knows how you function and he knows what's good for you.

IT'S NOT GOOD TO BE ALONE: CONNECTING WITH OTHERS

Whether we are single or married, we are called to do this life with others. More than thirty verses in the Bible talk about the importance of community — of meeting together, praying together, eating together, and living interconnected with other human beings.

I took a trip to the Middle East during which I had the opportunity to speak to a large group of young adults at one of the church meetings. To my surprise, I noticed that the youth there were not as obsessed with relationships with the opposite sex as the youth back home were. Don't get me wrong, they were typical young adults who desired one day to be married, but they did not share our fear of singleness.

I realized something profound. The youth there were living a completely different way than back home in the US. They lived in full-blown community. Their culture fostered togetherness, family, and friendship as the center of their lives. They worshiped and prayed together, ate and played together, visited each other and shared their lives. The fear of being alone was constantly trumped by togetherness. They fulfilled each other's need for love and connection.

I wonder if we in the West have missed something. What if we struggle with loneliness because we were never meant to be alone? What if our loneliness is the result not simply of needing a partner but of needing people? We are made in the image of a relational God; it makes sense that we possess the desire to be together.

Rather than telling singles to "love Jesus more" during their singleness, what if we were to offer them more love? Rather than obsessing about being alone, what if singles pursued community? If we were never meant to be alone, then why do we continue to live that way? Community doesn't just come to you; you have to seek it. Reach out and connect with those around you. Join with the body of believers and say no to discouragement and isolation.

IT'S NOT GOOD TO BE ALONE: CONNECTING WITH GOD

It's no coincidence that the greatest commandment in the Bible has three components: love God, love others, love yourself. As much as we need community, and as important as it is to get to know and love ourselves, what connects these things is our relationship with God. We were not made to be alone because ultimately we were made to love and connect with him.

One benefit of singleness is that I learned how to experience God in the most relational way. He went from being theoretically part of my life, to legitimately and practically part of my life. I learned to talk to him, to hang out with him, and to interact with him like never before. I needed to connect, and some days, he was the only one I had to connect with. I learned that he was always up for hanging out, and he proved to be real good company.

But maybe deep down you are wondering whether God really cares that you are alone. Maybe you are questioning his love for you, asking why he has left you to struggle through your singleness. Why has he left your prayers unanswered? Why doesn't he fill the void when you're feeling alone? What do you do when you're simply in need of love?

While Jesus may never become your significant other, he can become your significance, your serenity, and even your satisfaction.

FOUR KINDS OF LOVE

Have you ever noticed that in our society, the word *love* is used for so many different things? We say we love our family, and in the next breath declare our love for ice cream. *Love* loses its value when we use it in so many different contexts — from sports teams to romance to friendship to faith. The Greeks understood this, and instead of using a broad term for love, they used several terms to distinguish different kinds of love.

Scripture uses four Greek words for love. The first word is *storge*. This is the love of natural affection, as in the deep love of a parent for a child. It's a love that desires to give more than it desires to receive.

The second word for love in Scripture is *phileo*. I remember this word because it reminds me of the home of my favorite sports teams: Philadelphia, also known as the City of Brotherly Love. While there might not be any such love in this city during a heated football game, the Bible uses this word to refer to just that concept — brotherly love. It's the love of one friend for another, the love of one family member for another. It includes a sense of loyalty, camaraderie, and commitment.

The third kind of love is *eros*, from which we get the modern-day word *erotic*. This is romantic love and passion, a sensual love made up of desire. It is a deep attraction to the body, soul, and spirit of another. It may or may not include sexual desire, but it is a longing for a person as the object of one's affections.

The fourth love is *agape*. It is by far the greatest and deepest of all loves. It is in fact the very definition of true love in that it is unrelenting and unconditional. It is deeper than all of the other loves because it knows no limits. It is a divine love that gives because it wants to. It is a love that goes to the very ends of the earth in order to give, even giving its very self. The Bible uses this term to describe God's ferocious love toward mankind, a love that surpasses all understanding because it absolutely makes no sense. It is a love that is healing, full, and complete.

So many single young men and women are searching for a love to fill a void inside. And *eros* seems ready-made to fill it. It immediately seems to fulfill your longing and leaves you feeling intoxicated. But what if this void was never meant to be filled by a soul mate? What if it is just a sign to lead us toward something greater, a love even truer? Perhaps our ambiguous use of the word *love* has left us unaware of what we really need. What if we have been living to fill this void with *eros*, when the only thing that can suffice is *agape*?

There is something glorious about finding a soul mate. But there is a longing inside of us that can be satisfied only by the embrace of a True Lover: the God who loves us in the truest sense of the word. You cannot even begin to understand your need for love, much less learn to love others, until you have experienced the heart of this Lover. He longs to wrap you in his deep *agape* love. He desires to lavish it upon you unconditionally. He wants to give you this love because that's what he does, because loving you is what he wants to do.

THE BIG LETDOWN

Without realizing it, we idolize romantic love. We put it on a pedestal where it doesn't belong. As I look back on my life, I see a long series of letdowns as I put my hope in people and things that ultimately failed me. Friendships, jobs, guys I dated — each one fell short of my expectations.

But marriage, I thought, marriage would be different.

They say that the first year of marriage can be one of the most trying for many young couples. For John and me, that wasn't the case. Our first year was easily our honeymoon year, full of passion, romance, and spontaneity.

But eventually reality hit us, and we realized that marriage is a lifelong relationship between two selfish, flawed, and sinful people. Even in the midst of our intense love for one another, we were capable of hurting each other deeply and letting each other down. Arguments, annoyances, and misunderstandings, pet peeves, quirks, and personality differences — all rubbing up against each other, day after day after day.

You can put so much of your hope in one person. You can love them, commit to them, and trust them. But in the end, they can let you down, fail you, and hurt you. It's as though you give everything you have to this one thing, putting it above all other things, only to realize that it was never meant to have first place in your life. It doesn't belong there.

Don't get me wrong, a healthy marriage is one of the greatest blessings on earth. I wouldn't have written this book if I didn't believe that to be true. But as much as I cherish my husband and treasure our relationship, the truth is that even the most amazing marital love will let you down. It's so easy to forget this truth. It's so easy to keep putting your hope in the tangible, forgetting that it is only your faith in the unseen that is eternally satisfying. It's so easy to forget and forsake your first Love (Rev. 2:4).

THE TRUEST LOVE

Agape love has the power to exceed all expectations because it is a permanent love, a love that never disappoints, never diminishes, and never dies. Nothing can separate us from it. "For I am convinced that neither death nor life, neither angels nor demons, neither the present nor the future, nor any powers, neither height nor depth, nor anything else in all creation, will be able to separate us from the [*agape*] of God that is in Christ Jesus our Lord" (Rom. 8:38 – 39).

Agape was made for us, and we for *agape*. We will be searching for unconditional love until we find it here. St. Augustine speaks of this longing when he says of God, "Thou hast made us for Thyself and our hearts are restless until they rest in Thee."

Singleness can be so difficult to endure because you feel such an unrelenting ache for deep connection with another. Sometimes the wait seems eternal, and the future

> **FAQ 25**
> Does God have only one person in mind for me?

unknowable. For some of you, the wait is almost over. For others, it may last months or years or even a lifetime. While God's *agape* may never fill your void for *eros*, his unconditional love and affection can certainly comfort you, strengthen you, and enliven you. He is longing to open the floodgates and allow his love to pour down all over you.

The result of immersing yourself in God's love is that it requires you to trust — trust in a God who loves you enough to meet all of your needs, trust in a God who knows what is best for your life, trust in the one who promises that his will is good, pleasing, and perfect (Rom. 12:2), trust in a God whose love is matchless.

> Oh the deep, deep love of Jesus
> Vast, unmeasured, boundless, free
> Rolling as a mighty ocean
> In its fullness over me
>
> Underneath me, all around me
> Is the current of Your love
> Leading onward, leading homeward
> To Your glorious rest above
>
> — Samuel Trevor Francis,
> "Oh, the Deep Love of Jesus"

The deep love of our God is the only love that can lead you onward through this journey of life. But more than that, it is a love that will lead you inward — guiding you to the heart of who you are and who God has made you to be. It is a love that will lead you outward, giving you wisdom and peace as you engage in relationships in search of the love of your life. And more than anything, it is a love that will lead your heart upward, fixed on a God who will join you at your table for one, giving you comfort, joy, and peace as he pours his love on you. It's time to make room at your table, because you don't have to be alone. True Love is right here waiting.

Questions for Reflection

1. What is your attitude toward singleness?

2. What relationships exemplify the four kinds of love in your life? Out of the four kinds of love, is there a specific love that you need to continue to develop?

3. Have you been able to fully accept God's *agape* love for you? If not, what is keeping you from receiving this love?

4. Where are you on your journey of dating inward, outward, and upward?

PART FOUR

ASK THE COUNSELOR

CHAPTER 13

DATING INWARD, OUTWARD, UPWARD FAQS

1. Does God want me to be single forever?
2. What are some practical ways to date inward?
3. My parents are divorced and have always had a rocky marriage. I've heard divorce runs in families. Am I destined to go down this road as well?
4. How do I know whether I am in a toxic relationship?
5. How do I know whether I need professional counseling to help me work through my past?
6. Do your career aspirations need to line up with your partner's in order to have a healthy relationship?
7. How do cultural differences impact a relationship?
8. Do you believe in love at first sight?
9. What does the Bible have to say about dating?
10. Why do I always find myself in unhealthy relationships?
11. I just started dating this really nice guy/girl. But I don't feel that head-over-heels feeling. What should I do?
12. The person I have a romantic interest in has told me that our friendship will only ever be just that. How do I deal with being "just friends"?
13. My friend and I seem to be developing romantic feelings for one another. I've heard that dating a friend of the opposite

sex may be the best way to ruin a friendship. I really value our friendship. Is it worth the risk?

14. How do I know whether I am struggling with commitment issues?

15. Speaking of guarding your heart, is it okay for a woman to make the first move?

16. What are some questions that I can use to get to know someone better at the three levels of communication?

17. Can my sexual past affect my future relationships?

18. I know going all the way can be damaging to a relationship, but how far is too far?

19. I am dating a Christian, but our spirituality never seems to come up. What do I do?

20. Is it okay for a Christian to date a non-Christian?

21. What about "missionary dating"?

22. How do I deal with insecurities in a relationship?

23. Should you ever date someone you wouldn't consider marrying?

24. How do I deal with the pain of a breakup?

25. Does God have only one person in mind for me?

1. Does God want me to be single forever?

One of our greatest fears is the prospect of being single and alone forever. It's a thought that probably crosses the mind of every young adult at some point in their life. I recall wondering the same thing myself.

Though a lifetime of singleness is a possibility, statistically it isn't probable. But rather than gaining peace from statistics, it would be better to put your hope in God's promises.

A continuous source of encouragement to me during my single years was a verse found in Psalm 37: "Take delight in the LORD, and he will give you the desires of your heart" (v. 4).

For a time I interpreted this verse simply to mean that God would grant me what I wanted in life. You name it, he'll grant it, like having my very own genie in a bottle. While I have matured out of this perspective of a vending-machine God, when I became a parent I realized that there is some truth to this interpretation. Just as I delight in giving my children good things, our heavenly Father loves us and wants to give his children what they desire. But I also have come to understand that this verse is far deeper than that, because sometimes my perception of what is good for me is very different from God's perspective.

I heard another interpretation of this verse that really hit home for me. A pastor explained that when you delight in the Lord, he will *give* you your desires. He will place godly desires within you.

That was a transformational thought for me. It was freeing because it meant that if I really took to heart the practice of delighting in God as the love of my life, he would arrange my desires to line up with his. When you take joy in your relationship with God, you will find that you know him in a deeper way and, in turn, desire what he wants for your life. The almighty God's desires will be placed within you.

St. Augustine said it this way: "Love God and do what you want." This statement doesn't give us permission to do whatever we want in life. But it does mean that when we love God with our heart, soul, mind, and strength, our desires will align with his. Ultimately, what we choose to do as a result of following our desires will be aligned with his will.

It's important to understand that delighting in the Lord is not something you can just accomplish overnight. It's a process. More than that, it's a relationship, and it takes time, energy, commitment, and a whole lot of communication to really understand someone's heart. God wants you to get to know him with at least the same passion with which you desire to get to know your future mate.

Speaking of mates, it's a myth to think that all joys will be fulfilled the moment you meet your future spouse. God wants us to learn how to take joy in him because no matter where this life takes us, be it down the road of singleness or on the path of marriage, true joy can be found only in relationship with him.

I am married to an incredible man, but I can tell you that there are days when he lets me down, and I guarantee you he'd say the same about me. Though we love each other deeply, complete joy doesn't come from the love between us; it comes from the love we receive from our Lord, a love that we delight in and live for, a love that overflows into every part of our lives and, in turn, into our relationship with each other. It is that first love for God that drives a thriving marriage.

If you desire marriage, seek God. If you desire singleness, seek God. In the end, if you entrust your heart to him, God will use your desires to lead you in the right direction. Just as I believe marriage is a calling, I also believe singleness is a calling, one that God will equip you for if he calls you to it. For now, delight in God, give your heart to him, and then allow him to lead your desires. He can be trusted. He knows what is best for your life. He will not let you down.

2. What are some practical ways to date inward?

Taking yourself to dinner and a movie is not what I mean by dating inward, though I suppose it could be an insightful experience. The bottom line is that dating inward is not an action that you do but rather an experience that you invest in as often as you are able and willing. Dating inward means taking the time and energy to learn about who you are.

As I mentioned at the end of chapter 3, a great way to get to know yourself is through journaling. Journaling is a way to keep track of your internal dialogue; it's a way of communicating with yourself. It's important to track your thoughts, feelings, behaviors, experiences, and interactions to help you observe yourself from the inside out. As a friend of mine put it, "It took me until my late twenties to figure out how to 'date inward,' and only with God's help. I remember coming to that point in my late twenties — finally figuring out who I was and then being able to take that into my relationships rather than trying to fit myself into 'working right' with a certain person. For a long time I thought I had to change to make a relationship work instead of being myself in the relationship God wanted me in."

Focus on whom God has made you to be, rather than on whom he has made for you to be with. Here are some questions to help you start the process of dating inward:

1. How are my relationships with my family members?
2. Do any of those relationships need healing, forgiveness, or confrontation?
3. What are the positive values and traits I have learned from my family of origin? What are the negative ones?
4. What in my past has shaped me in a harmful way?
5. What in my past has caused emotional damage?
6. What are some words that describe me?
7. What are my talents, strengths, and skills?
8. How do I feel about my body?
9. What habits in my life are harmful or unhealthy?
10. How do I approach interactions with others?
11. What situations make me feel the most defensive? Angry? Stressed?
12. How do I deal with and express my emotions?
13. What things do I think about the most? What things do I talk about the most?

14. Do I value myself? How would I describe my self-esteem?
15. Am I more of a listener or a talker? Do I need to work on either area?
16. What are some things I hope to accomplish? Am I on the right track? If not, what is holding me back?
17. What is on my bucket list?
18. What are my goals?
19. What do I think is my life's calling, purpose, or mission?
20. What am I passionate about? What am I good at?
21. How would I describe my spiritual life and personal relationship with God?
22. How have I grown spiritually over the past year? What has been keeping me from growing?
23. Where have I seen God at work in my life?
24. How much and how often do I communicate with God?
25. In what ways do I communicate with God?
26. What spiritual disciplines do I need to improve on?
27. In what areas of my life do I need God's forgiveness?
28. In what areas of my life do I need to forgive myself?

3. My parents are divorced and have always had a rocky marriage. I've heard divorce runs in families. Am I destined to go down this road as well?

It is true that you tend to follow the patterns that you experience in your family of origin. Those whose parents have divorced or who have witnessed their parents' tumultuous relationship might acquire a tainted perspective on marriage. They may be cynical toward the ideas of commitment, loyalty, and trust. They may fear intimacy with others, having seen the devastating results of it in their parents' relationship. They may harbor hurt, resentment, and fear. The unfortunate reality is that children who have witnessed divorce carry the negative effects of that broken relationship as part of their psychological makeup.

But thankfully, though divorce may leave emotional wounds, it is in no way hereditary. There is no gene that determines your level of commitment and loyalty in marriage. You always have a choice.

In this generation of instant gratification and living for the moment, we shouldn't be surprised that the divorce rate is so high for both Christians and non-Christians alike. In our culture, we seem to believe the lie that we should do what feels good in the moment, and falling out of love seems just as unintentional as falling in love. When love fails to satisfy, we think it's normal to walk away and never look back.

The Bible explains that God "hates divorce" (Mal. 2:16). It's not because he is a dictator looking down in anger and disgust at broken marriages; it is because he knows how much it hurts. Divorce causes pain, brokenness, and permanent damage to God's people, something he never wants them to go through. He hates divorce because it grieves his heart and the hearts of his children. Though the Bible grants a couple of exceptions,[9] it presents an overwhelming amount of encouragement to hold on to your spouse and the vows you made before God.

As with all meaningful things in life, staying married is a deliberate decision. But more than that, it is a series of decisions that begins during singleness and continues throughout dating. It is time and time again choosing what is right over what feels good, what is healthy over what is fun. It begins with a commitment to yourself, your values, your future, and your God. And ultimately, it is a decision to choose the right partner and to remain true, loyal, and committed no matter what obstacles you may face along the way.

You are not destined to follow in the footsteps of your parents, or anyone else for that matter, but you must choose to walk a different way. Be deliberate and choose faithfulness, loyalty, and commitment in the decisions you make today and every single day.

4. How do I know whether I am in a toxic relationship?

As a therapist, I've heard my share of painful stories. Broken hearts, hurting people, and dysfunctional relationships are a lot more common than anyone could ever guess. Even so, people don't like to talk about toxic relationships. Unfortunately, closing our eyes to them only increases their prevalence. The truth is that they exist everywhere, all over the world, and they exist among Christians as well.

Rather than just deny the existence of toxic relationships, it's time to start the conversation and get in tune with the healing that needs to take place.

Toxic relationships tear down, rather than build up. Their poison can manifest in different forms, but the result is always the same: a cycle of pain, pain, and more pain. Take a look at the following characteristics of toxic relationships to assess whether your relationship might be toxic:

- *Emotionally toxic.* The emotional atmosphere in a relationship determines how healthy the relationship is. An emotionally toxic relationship continuously creates a spiral of negative feelings. It involves the painful aftermath of problems such as cheating, suicidal threats, rage, jealousy, isolation, manipulation, or control. In an emotionally toxic relationship, one's partner exhibits a cycle of breaking trust time and time again.
- *Mentally toxic.* Mentally toxic relationships plant seeds of negativity in your mind. Your partner puts you down and criticizes you rather than lifts you up and encourages you. This verbal abuse includes constant criticism, dishonesty, cursing, name-calling, and degrading. In a mentally toxic relationship, your partner devalues you and tears you down.
- *Physically toxic.* When people think of a toxic relationship,

they typically think of a physically toxic relationship. Many toxic relationships begin with emotional and mental components and slowly make their way into the physical — manipulation and control by way of bodily harm. This includes hitting, kicking, slapping, spitting, pushing, and shoving. In a physically toxic relationship, one's partner uses their hands and bodies for destruction and devastation, not as instruments of healing.

• *Sexually toxic.* A sexually toxic relationship leads you into sexual acts that leave you feeling guilt and shame. In such relationships, the majority of the relationship is centered on sexual experience. Sometimes sexually toxic relationships include forced and manipulated sexual acts. Sexually toxic relationships erode the meaning of sex, using it as a tool for selfish gain and pleasure.

• *Spiritually toxic.* There are two kinds of spiritually toxic relationships. The first is a relationship with someone who stands outside of your religious beliefs, typically someone who does not respect your faith and spirituality. This person's behavior could include verbally degrading your beliefs and dishonoring your values by doing things around you that you aren't comfortable with. It's a passive toxicity in that it distracts you, discourages you, and corrodes your relationship with God.

The second kind of spiritually toxic relationship is manipulative, controlling, and legalistic. In such a relationship, your partner uses religion falsely to control you into submitting to their will. Claiming to know God's will, this kind of partner often encourages you to trust them instead of trusting God. They use guilt and fear to gain power, and they twist God's Word to promote abuse, injustice, and selfish gain within the relationship.

All of these types of toxic relationships are deadly in that they always draw you away from God's unconditional love instead of pushing you toward it. They are founded on selfishness, control, and restrictions rather than humility, trust, and freedom.

Examine your relationship and ask whether it is edifying, honoring, and uplifting. We are called to be in relationships in which we are exchanging hope and spreading God's love like a contagious disease. Don't ever settle for less than true love. Believe that you were made for so much more than this.

For more information, see "FAQ 10: Why do I always find myself in unhealthy relationships?" Also, for assistance in breaking free of a toxic relationship, go to the website of the American Association of Christian Counselors (www.aacc.net) to find professional help in your area.

5. How do I know whether I need professional counseling to help me work through my past?

First things first — let me clarify what counseling is not. Counseling is not a time of meditative relaxation while lying on the couch of a bearded psychologist who analyzes the details of your childhood dreams. It's not a conversation that consists of repeatedly answering the question "How does that make you feel?" It's also not a series of mystical tests in which you are asked to express the depths of your unconscious while staring at various ink blots.

Counseling is an ongoing conversation with a professional by which you gain insight, perspective, and growth. It is a relationship with a therapist that allows transparency and authenticity to take root in your heart and in your life. It is an opportunity to accumulate new ideas and information that may have huge implications on your understanding of the past and in turn transform your present. And ultimately, it is taking part in hope and healing for your life.

Counseling is not for "crazies," as the old and quickly dying stigma once implied. On the contrary, it is for strong and courageous men and women who realize that their habits, hurts, and hang-ups are preventing them from living the lives they want to live. No matter how big or small your struggle, here are some things to consider as you contemplate the benefits of counseling:

1. Do I find myself caught in patterns, habits, or addictions that I can't seem to break free from, no matter how hard I try?
2. Do feelings of anxiety and/or depression affect me more days than not?
3. Is this present or past situation getting in the way of my ability to function socially (romantic relationships, family, friends), or affecting my productivity at work or school?
4. Is my mental or emotional world affecting my physical body? (Sleep, lack of concentration, appetite changes, energy levels, etc.)

If you answered yes to one or more of these questions, consider getting professional counseling to help you on your journey of healing and recovery. You were created to live an abundant life; don't let the wounds of your past or the struggles of your present keep you from living fully.

6. Do your career aspirations need to line up with your partner's in order to have a healthy relationship?

I met a musician who was determined that she would never marry anyone outside of the music industry. She claimed that being in the industry necessitated a way of life that she could not compromise for someone who didn't understand the culture. For her, career aspirations were top priority in finding a relationship.

Conversely, I have a friend who works as a nurse who swore she would never date or marry someone in her line of work. She wanted to be in a relationship with someone who could talk about subjects other than medicine and patient care. She wanted someone with his own strengths and skills who would compliment her rather than compete with her.

Each person has to come to their own conclusion regarding the role of career aspirations in a relationship.

More important than having identical career aspirations is sharing a similar lifestyle. Think about your lifestyle and then consider your hopes for the future. For example, if you despise traveling and a constantly changing environment, then you should consider the price of dating someone whose career calls for regular travel and frequent relocation.

Anna and Rick did not think through these things as high school seniors. They were married shortly after graduation, and three years later they came to see me with seemingly irreconcilable differences. Rick was a traditional young man. He grew up with a stay-at-home mom who took care of him and his brothers, so it was important to him that his wife would do the same for their children. Anna had a different opinion. She was a free spirit who believed that women should not be stuck at home "barefoot and pregnant," as she called it, but instead should pursue their full potential. Her career was top on her priority list, and she started her own business to prove her independence and to pursue her dreams. This couple's opposing lifestyle beliefs had worn on their marriage. Rick was disappointed in Anna's lack of "family values," while Anna believed that Rick was holding her back.

The moral of this story is that lifestyle values have a significant effect on a relationship. The greater the difference between two people's lifestyle preferences, the more relational stress there will be.

Search for someone who believes in your passions and appreciates your goals, who understands your long-term perspective and acknowledges the sacrifices that it will entail. Find someone who has realistic expectations and is ready for the give-and-take that comes when two people with separate lives are joined. And just as important as finding such a person is becoming a person like this yourself.

7. How do cultural differences impact a relationship?

I was out to dinner with some of my girlfriends when in the course of the conversation it was observed that three out of the four of us were in interracial marriages. The conversation turned to the joys and obstacles of being married to someone from another race or culture.

My friends would vouch for the truth that cultural differences in a relationship can challenge you, widening your horizons through exposure to experiences and ideas you otherwise never would have encountered. There is much to be discovered by seeing the world through the eyes of another, which is why in so many cases, people who are different from each other tend to attract. But even so, before entering any relationship, it's important to consider the price of each difference, making sure that it is an investment you are willing to make.

One thing my friends observed is that some of the stressors that they face are external. We live in a society that still hasn't fully accepted the value of diversity. One of the hardest obstacles they had ever faced was dealing with people — Christians and non-Christians alike — who tried to convince them that their relationship would not be acceptable to God. Some even misquoted the Scripture about being "unequally yoked" as a way to keep them from joining in marriage. Thankfully, the closed-mindedness of certain family members and friends did not keep them from seeing that though they were different, they were made for each other, and they are each happily married today.

Having said that, my friends also would acknowledge that in addition to social prejudice, intercultural relationships have a unique set of obstacles, because a person's culture shapes their view of life and relationships. Language, gender roles, time management, communication style, personal space, family values, and body language are just some of the things that can be shaped by a person's cultural background. When two cultures come together in a marriage relationship, conflict can arise in all of these areas.

My friend is married into a Middle Eastern family. If you know anything about the Middle Eastern culture, it puts little priority on time management. (Being Middle Eastern myself, I know from firsthand experience!) Relationships and socializing are far more important than schedules and efficiency, and so, being late is common. In fact, if you're planning to schedule an event at noon, be prepared for everyone to arrive closer to 1:00 or 2:00 p.m. As small as this cultural difference may seem, for my efficient American friend, the prospect of being late to pretty much everything began to wear thin on him, and almost every outing turned into an argument. This cultural difference became a big source of stress in their relationship.

While intercultural relationships can be enriching, it's important to have a healthy understanding of what they will entail. Be sure to acknowledge and understand your differences, and then invest the time that it takes to work through the joys and obstacles that come with each one.

8. Do you believe in love at first sight?

Boy meets girl. They instantly fall in love. And live happily ever after. Love at first sight. It's such a romantic idea. It's what Hollywood movies are made of. But beyond the romance of Hollywood, is there truly such a thing as love at first sight?

Many people vouch for this idea. According to them, they knew they had met their soul mate within a few moments of making eye contact. Their feelings were undeniable. The heart-fluttering, browsweating, stomach-knotting emotions were simply out of their control.

They were struck by the "disease" of love, and there was nothing they could do to get over it. So, they ask, how can one explain this instant connection other than by saying that it is pure love?

I'm always hesitant to endorse the idea of love at first sight, because it defines love as a feeling, and the truth is that feelings cannot always be trusted. Feelings come, and feelings go. One minute we are sad, and then in a blink of an eye, happiness follows. Confusion turns to assurance. Excitement into fear. Feelings can influence us, but they should never lead the way. To believe in love at first sight is essentially to let emotions take the reins, which ultimately causes devastation and heartbreak more than it makes a way for romance.

On the other hand, feelings should never be repressed. They are meaningful when kept in perspective. They have an important place in our lives and can be a powerful influence in the choices that we make.

It's crucial to distinguish between the feelings of love and the actions of love. Though we might feel the feelings of love, which I prefer to call attraction, upon first glance, those feelings are not the actions of love.

My husband, John, describes his first encounter with me as an instant attraction. He says he walked into the room and was "overwhelmingly struck" by my beauty. He couldn't take his eyes off of me. Something inexplicable drew him to me. But though his emotions were a first step toward love, they were not love itself. Love is defined by what a person does, rather than just how they feel.

The greatest definition of love ever written is found in the pages of the Bible. The Bible reveals love as a choice that is based not entirely on a feeling but on the commitment of one person to another. Love is a giving of self with no expectation to receive, a decision made every moment of every day. It is the reality of unconditional love. "Love is patient, love is kind. It does not envy, it does not boast, it is not proud. It does not dishonor others, it is not self-seeking, it is not easily angered, it keeps no record of wrongs. Love does not delight in evil but rejoices with the truth. It always protects, always trusts, always hopes, always perseveres. Love never fails" (1 Cor. 13:4 – 8). According to this passage, true love is a series of actions and a pattern of choices. But what's even more amazing is that this definition comes from a God who took it upon himself to show us what choosing love means. He gave complete love by pursuing it as an action — to the point of sacrificing his life.

Love at first sight is never complete love, because it is based on an emotion rather than a commitment, a feeling rather than a choice. True love is born when two people commit to offer themselves for the sake of the other person. It is a process of growth that deepens a couple's bond.

And that's exactly what happened with John and me. The instant attraction slowly grew into something deeper, something more meaningful. We chose to connect with, to give to, to serve, and to honor one another in the relationship that formed thereafter. Our every decision from that time on watered the seed of love. Attraction may have opened the door, but action kept it open. And love was born. True love. Real love. Lasting love. Because stronger than love at first sight is choosing love thereafter.

9. What does the Bible have to say about dating?

There are many significant topics about which the Bible has little or nothing to say. Modern times have introduced concepts that did not exist in ancient days and that in some countries do not yet exist even today. Dating is one of those topics.

I have to laugh to myself when I hear people say that they want to date "biblically," because that would look a whole lot different from the dating that we see today. Parents of the bride would select an eligible bachelor and betroth their daughter with a dowry (valued treasures that the family of the bride gives to the groom). Parents, dowries, and donkeys — I'd say dating biblically could make for an awkward modern-day rendezvous at Starbucks.

So who's still up for dating "biblically"?

It seems as though the cultural norms of the day set the stage for the development of relationships. Though it may not be possible to date biblically, it's still possible to date in a way that honors God no matter the cultural norms. The Bible doesn't talk directly about dating, but it does speak volumes about relationships, godly interactions, and principles that can be applied to how you date.

As Christians, we are called to build up, honor, and respect the people we interact with (1 Thess. 5:11). We're asked to keep people in our lives who have good values and who are kindred spirits (1 Cor. 15:33). We're warned not to get too close to those who aren't connected with God (2 Cor. 6:14).

Though the Bible doesn't give us rules and regulations about dating, we're to be guided by the underlying principle of loving and honoring God, allowing our lives to point to him in every single thing that we do (1 Cor. 10:31), dating included. The Bible makes it clear that life is less about the "do's" and "don'ts" and so much more about doing what's beneficial, healthy, and righteous (1 Cor. 10:23). Scripture can guide us to date in a way that honors God and others.

10. Why do I always find myself in unhealthy relationships?

This question is the cry of many young men and women who come to my office for relationship help. For some, these unhealthy relationships involve a partner who is withdrawn and distracted; for others, it's a partner who is aggressive and abusive. For many, these relationships involve addictions that run the spectrum from alcoholism to workaholism. As Robin Norwood notes in her book *Women Who Love Too Much*, for all of these young men and women, these relationships involve a partner who is in some way emotionally unavailable.

Rita could not understand why it was so difficult for her to break up with Andre once and for all. She had heard of women who were stuck in abusive relationships, and she couldn't face the fact that this was now her story. Somehow, she had ended up in a relationship in which she was mistreated, lied to, and verbally degraded. All she had wanted was to feel loved and accepted, but this need had brought her to a dangerous place.

We were born with the desire for love and affirmation. For young men and women who grow up in healthy families, this need is met through the parents' loving words, affectionate touch, gentle presence, and fulfillment of emotional needs. But for men and women like Rita, the ache for affirmation and love is never fulfilled. For them, emotionally unavailable parents were the norm.

Emotional unavailability can take on many different forms: mothers who are distant and withdrawn, preoccupied with their own burdens; fathers who are aggressive and abusive, overtaken by longstanding addictions — parents who are so absorbed by their own issues that they ignore the needs of their children. In every case, deep-seated emotional needs are left unfulfilled.

For many people, romantic relationships become the avenue by which to pacify unmet emotional needs. Through them, they can "reenact" the interactions of their past, change now what they couldn't change then, and gain what was never offered in their family of origin.

And so the cycle of toxic relationships begins — a pursuit of the emotionally unavailable partner, in the hope of gaining from them what could not be gained from their past, in the hope of changing them, in the hope of winning them over with their love.

The sad reality is that these relationships, though many times passionate and exciting, are also chaotic and unstable. In the end, they never bring the fulfillment our hearts long for, because they cannot. They end in pain, brokenness, and shattered trust.

But for the determined, there is hope of becoming free from toxic relationships:

1. *Come to terms with your needs.* One great way to begin this process is by writing in a journal a few times a week. Keep track of your feelings, from things that hurt you to things that excite you. Take the time to get to know yourself and understand your emotional needs.

2. *Bring these needs before God.* Some people may be able to make amends with their family members, but for others, this is not a realistic goal. The good news is that healing and forgiveness can come with or without the consent of the one who hurt you. Ask God to grant you the ability to forgive, and then ask him to meet your needs for value, love, and affirmation through his Word. The Bible is filled with affirmations about who we are in Christ. Take those words in, memorize them, and allow them to be a daily part of your life.

3. *Find some friends to hold you accountable.* List the reasons why you have decided to take steps toward change, and find some godly friends, family members, or pastors or church leaders of the same sex to help walk you through this journey. Give each of them a copy of your list, and when you need a little reminder, call them up or schedule a time to meet with them to discuss your struggles and your successes. Consider seeking professional counseling as an added branch of accountability and as a source of new perspective.

4. *Break away.* Follow through with the changes you have decided to make. Bring closure to the relationships that have been keeping you from God's best for your life. If any

type of verbal, physical, or emotional abuse is involved, please see a professional counselor who can guide you in taking the necessary steps to keep you safe. Surround yourself with friends and family who can support you through this hard time.

5. *Remember, this process is never easy.* It is always difficult letting go of the comfortable and familiar, even when it is harmful to us. Change can be a very scary thing. Even if you are motivated to take the right steps, don't expect it to be a walk in the park. Your emotions will play tricks on you; you will doubt yourself and wonder whether you have made the right choice. Take advantage of your accountability partners, and go to them for extra strength.

God is longing to free you from the cycle of toxic relationships. He is longing to fill the needs of your heart. He is longing to renew your mind and open your heart to the great things he has in store for your life. Every step toward letting go of your unhealthy relationships will free you to step forward into a better life.

11. I just started dating this really nice guy/girl. But I don't feel that head-over-heels feeling. What should I do?

Out of all of the frequently asked questions in this book, this is the one I'm asked most often. It's an important question, but before I can answer it, we need to define a couple of terms.

Head-over-heels feeling: an exaggerated response to seeing, interacting with, or being in the presence of someone of the opposite sex; a feeling of euphoria, stomach-dropping, or nervous energy associated with positive regard.

Attraction: the response of being drawn to someone physically, mentally, and emotionally; possessing a strong desire to be with a particular individual, longing for connection, investment, and intimacy.

I tend to give the head-over-heels feeling little weight. One reader explained his dilemma this way: "I've been dating this wonderful girl for about two months now. She has everything that I'm looking for, including the core values (born again, conservative, doesn't drink, wants to strive for purity, etc.). And she is gorgeous! What I don't understand is, why don't I get 'that feeling' that I get from just looking at other girls whom I've never even met before? How important is that 'head-over-heels feeling' when you first start dating someone? If you don't start feeling it after a few months of dating, does that signal a problem, even if the relationship is going well?"

To this young man, I would stress the difference between a head-over-heels feeling and attraction. When it comes to feeling chemistry in a relationship, many times we have unrealistic expectations. Add to that the unfortunate influence of our entertainment and media — sexual images, and storylines featuring lust and infatuation — and we're sure to be disappointed in the real world.

The most interesting thing I've observed about the head-over-heels feeling is that it is many times rooted in anxiety. It's the stomach-sinking, heart-racing, sweat-producing, mouth-drying adrenaline rush of encountering the mysterious and the unknown, that awkwardly exciting infatuation that comes with the novelty of a new relationship. Ironically, it's a symptom of fear.

But in healthy relationships, there is no room for fear. First John 4:18 explains that "there is no fear in love. But perfect love drives out fear."

There may be no room for fear in love, but there is always room for attraction. Attraction is the mutual drawing of two human beings to one another. It signals affection, connection, and interest that is sometimes subtle — and sometimes strong. It is the precursor to all that is good in a relationship, leading two people to establish intimacy and exclusivity within their relationship. Attraction is important; in fact, it's crucial. But it must never be confused with that head-over-heels feeling.

Feelings come and go, but relationships that are founded on attraction draw two people together physically, emotionally, and mentally. It's important to feel an attraction that draws you deeper into the relationship and keeps you excited about what's to come. Keep your eye out for that kind of connection, and then hold on to it tight.

For more on healthy attraction, see chapter 6.

12. The person I have a romantic interest in has told me that our friendship will only ever be just that. How do I deal with being "just friends"?

You thought there were sparks between you: a subtle smile, a quick glance across the room, a good conversation. You may have even spent some quality time together, talking, laughing, and enjoying each other's company. Finally, you decided to put your feelings out there, hoping to find mutual affection. Unfortunately, you were ushered into the dreaded friend zone. You bared your heart and soul only to find that sparks were not flying in both directions.

Oh, the "just friends" category. Sometimes a person would rather be enemies than be put in this little box.

So how are you supposed to react in this situation? Where can you go from here? Here are some things to consider if you've been placed in the friend zone:

1. *Maintain firm boundaries within your friendship.* One of the biggest mistakes people make in the "just friends"

category is blurring the line between friendship and dating, investing physically, emotionally, financially, or spiritually in someone who is not interested in dating them. Many people blur this line hoping that it might somehow usher them out of the friend zone and into the dating zone. But the opposite usually happens. A dating relationship never blossoms because the person you are interested in has no need to go there. If you grant someone the benefits of being in a relationship without their having to commit, why would they enter a dating relationship with you and do the relational work that is usually needed to earn those benefits? If you're called a friend, then be *just* a friend. Save your time and energy for someone who is ready for the commitment and work a relationship entails.

2. *Remember that only one person has to be the right match.* As difficult as it can be to be placed in the "just friends" category, it's important to see this zone as a blessing. Looking back on my life, I realize that my being put in the friend zone was one of the greatest blessings. Though at the time it really hurt to be rejected by the guy I was interested in, I didn't know that only a few months later I would be introduced to the man I would marry. The "just friends" category was God's way of getting me to stop fixating on the person I thought was right for me, leaving me available for the one who was my perfect match. Think of it this way: being just friends gives you one less person to consider in your search for your soul mate. Be at peace, because God's plans are always much better than your own.

3. *Find someone who is just as crazy about you as you are about them.* The thing about the "just friends" status is that it actually reveals a lot. It exposes the heart of a person who

isn't interested in pursuing a romantic relationship with you. Doesn't that say enough? At the end of the day, you want to be in a relationship with someone who is just as madly in love with you as you are with them. Consider the "just friends" tag a signal to just walk away and move forward, freeing you to pursue a relationship in which the romantic energy flows both ways. You deserve that. Wait for it.

4. *Remember that it's nearly impossible to backtrack to the "just friends" category* with someone for whom your heart has sprouted feelings. I've known many people who have tried to straddle the fence between friendship and romance only to find themselves falling onto the romantic side again and again and again, and then having to be ushered back into the friend zone every time, with more emotional bumps and bruises. Many good things can come of a friendship, but when you've found yourself at a dead end, do yourself a favor and put some distance in your friendship. Place a buffer zone around your interactions and limit your time together so that you don't find your feelings going where they don't have permission to go.

Though it may be painful, finding yourself in the "just friends" category can propel you into greater and more satisfying relationships in the future. Don't let it get you down, but learn to see its hidden blessings.

13. My friend and I seem to be developing romantic feelings for one another. I've heard that dating a friend of the opposite sex may be the best way to ruin a friendship. I really value our friendship. Is it worth the risk?

A good friendship is foundational to a healthy romantic relationship. While a friendship can be built in the presence of romance, romance can also find roots in the soil of a friendship. Some of the best relationships I know started that way.

Yet there's something intimidating about crossing the line between friendship and dating. It's a vulnerable place to be, baring your heart to acknowledge affections that might be more easily left unspoken. But there should be no better place to discuss something so "risky" than in the presence of a true friend.

Is it worth the risk to take the next step and date a friend? Ask yourself the following questions:

1. *Does this relationship have the qualities of a true friendship?* Real friends offer encouragement and support. They are genuine and honest, whether or not they agree with you. They are people you can trust and respect. If this sounds like your friendship, then it is likely a safe place to share your feelings and take the next step.

2. *Do you feel a romantic attraction to your friend?* Many Christians think of their friendships with the opposite sex as "brother-sister" relationships. It's an important way of thinking about the opposite sex because it keeps you grounded and leaves little room for inappropriate interactions. But as important as it is to feel comfortable in your friendship, it's just as important to feel a romantic attraction. Attraction is not what relationships are built on, but it propels relationships from one stage into the next. Consider your level of attraction before taking the next step.

3. *Are you willing to see the dynamics of your relationship change?* Pursuing relationships is risky. In this case, the risk is that the friendship will change. When a friendship develops to the point that it might become a romantic

relationship, something has to give — either give more or give less. On one hand, the friendship might transform into a romantic relationship — more affection, more time commitment, more dedication. On the other hand, the friendship might take a step back — less interaction, less investment, less involvement. It's a fork in the road that might redefine your friendship. But change can be a good thing, leading you to reprioritize your friendship and redefine your boundaries. Change can lead you into something wonderful, or prevent you from continuing on a dead-end road. Either way, it's a risk.

As with so many things in life, only you can decide whether the risk is worth taking.

14. How do I know whether I am struggling with commitment issues?

Trust is the root of commitment. When you pick a college, you trust that the college will deliver the educational opportunities that it promises. When you accept a job, you trust that your place of employment will function as your employer says it will. When you enter a relationship, you trust that the other person will respect you, honor you, and take care of your heart.

I've interacted with my share of people who are struggling with their ability to commit to a relationship. I find that there are two kinds of people.

The first are those who fear commitment because of whom they are committing to. Maybe they are dating someone who behaves in a way that is harmful to the relationship. Maybe they've experienced betrayal. Or maybe the person they are in relationship with is just not right for them, and they don't have peace about moving forward.

In these situations, the fear of commitment seems to be legitimate. A person is afraid to commit because they are not supposed to commit. Their experiences with their partner or their partner's behavior cause them to second-guess, to fear the next step. It's important to trust your instincts when you have such concerns in a relationship.

The second are those who fear commitment because of who they are. Many times, people are filled with unjustifiable fears. They may be in a relationship that is healthy and everything they ever wanted, but "for some reason or other," they are afraid to commit.

April was one of those people. Three years ago she had met Joshua, the kind of man she had always dreamed of marrying. He was a devoted Christian who actually walked his talk. He was passionate about God and he was crazy about her. He treated her with dignity, kindness, and respect. They had many things in common and found themselves talking for hours on end. They had fun together and enjoyed each other's company. But after three years of dating, she was still afraid. He had mentioned the prospect of getting engaged numerous times, but she continued to make excuses. "The timing isn't right." "Let's finish our education." "Maybe we should save some more money." Deep down, she was terrified to move forward.

When she was a child, April's dad had abandoned her and her mother. She woke up one Sunday morning to find her mom curled up in a ball in her bedroom, crying hysterically. With little explanation, April's dad had left for another woman he had fallen in love with.

Twenty years later, April found herself entertaining the same fears she felt as a child. What if she were abandoned again? Could she take the risk? Would she be able to bear the pain? Time and again Joshua had proved his consistency, loyalty, and patience, yet she was afraid to let her guard down. She was afraid to commit.

Maybe you too are in a wonderful healthy relationship, but pain from your past is keeping you from taking the next step. If so, you are not alone. Fears from the past prevent many people from moving forward. Commitment issues are a sign that emotional healing needs to take place in your life. If you find yourself struggling to commit to good things, it's time to identify what is holding you back and how to move forward. Since each situation is so personal, it's important to consult a professional counselor to help you remove the obstacles that are in your way. No matter how much pain is in your past, or how much fear is in your present, there is always hope for peace and security in your future.

To find a professional counselor in your area, go to www.aacc.net *and click on the "Find a Christian Counselor" tab.*

15. Speaking of guarding your heart, is it okay for a woman to make the first move?

Pick up any of the old dating books on my shelf and I'll guarantee you this — you won't find a single one that encourages women to get out there and make the first move. It's no secret that Christians are a little old-fashioned when it comes to love.

I grew up with the belief that a woman should never initiate a relationship, that the man should be the one to take the lead. The man is the pursuer and the woman is the object of pursuit. Many Christians believe that a man's leadership role begins at the moment of interest and continues throughout marriage.

My marriage is much different from what I once imagined it would be. During my dating years, I pictured the man leading the way and taking charge, the way the dating books said it should be. But as I matured, I wondered whether I could live with this one-sided view of relationships, and more important, I wondered whether it was even biblical. Scripture honors marriage and reinforces marital roles, but it seems that the biblical concept of a healthy marriage has nothing to do with who initiates the relationship. According to God's

Word, a healthy relationship has far more to do with the love that is exchanged within it than it does with who made the first move.

My husband and I have committed to a marriage in which we are both equal parts of the equation — challenging each other, correcting each other, sharpening each other, encouraging each other, and "submitting to one another" (Eph. 5:21). We may have distinct roles, but we still have a mutual relationship, respecting and honoring each other as equals.

I see the roots of our equality in our dating relationship, because what you see in dating, you will — one hundred percent of the time — see later in marriage. Throughout our dating relationship, we shared our feelings with one another. We each claim that we were the one to initiate, but what matters is not who initiated but how we responded thereafter. We both responded with affirming words and validating actions. We invested in the relationship equally, together giving and receiving. We kept communication open the whole way through.

More important than who initiates a relationship are the mutual love and respect that are exchanged from that point on. So is it okay for a woman to take the first step toward a relationship? Absolutely. But before you do, consider the following:

1. Have you prayed a lot about this relationship and felt the Lord's leading in this next step?
2. Do you see lots of healthy traits in the person you are interested in?
3. Have you sensed that he is interested in you? (Ask yourself why he hasn't initiated so far.)
4. Are you okay with getting turned down? (After you've let him know, you must be willing to let it go!)
5. How you act, react, and interact through dating indicates how you will act, react, and interact in marriage. Though

it's okay to initiate a relationship, it's not okay to fall into a pattern in which you are doing all of the work. Look for patterns of interaction that reflect mutual commitment, reciprocal feelings, and give-and-take between you and your partner.

6. Most important, if you are planning to initiate a conversation, you should always expect a response. It doesn't matter who starts the relationship with the first word, but it does matter that both people continue to invest in the relationship and pursue it equally through their actions, feelings, and words from that point forward. True love is a two way street!

For a biblical example of a woman initiating a relationship, check out the story of Ruth in the Bible.

16. What are some questions that I can use to get to know someone better at the three levels of communication?

Level 1 Conversation Starters:

1. What do you do for a living? Or, What are you studying?
2. Where did you grow up?
3. What do you do for fun?
4. How do you spend your time?

Level 2 Conversation Starters:

1. What are your dreams and aspirations?
2. What is your family like?
3. What do you like or dislike about your job? Career? Life?
4. What are your beliefs or opinions about [insert topic]?

Level 3 Conversation Starters:

1. What stresses you out?
2. When have you felt the most happy?
3. What are you passionate about?
4. What are you looking forward to or excited about?
5. What are you proud of?
6. What are your feelings about me?

17. Can my sexual past affect my future relationships?

Every decision we make inevitably has some impact on our relationships with others in the future. From the career we choose, to the hobbies we enjoy, to the friendships we invest in, our choices affect who we become and the impact we have on the world around us. Our sexual choices are no exception.

We are shaped by sex because we learn so much from sexual intimacy. In these intense emotional and physical moments, we are exposed to lessons on love, selflessness, communication, loyalty, and commitment — or the lack thereof. We learn to express and receive love. For many young men and women, these lessons are painful when a lack of commitment leads two bodies that once were united to go their separate ways.

I've met with many young adults who have shared about the impact their sexual experiences have had on their lives and, in turn, their relationships. Many have been left with psychological wounds, emotional attachments, and sexual expectations that were a direct result of their sexual experiences before marriage.

One young woman struggled to let go of the memories of past sexual encounters with other men that seemed to haunt her while she was engaging in sexual intimacy with her husband. She wanted to be freed from her past, to forgive herself, and to commit her mind and heart fully to her husband. But her sexual past seemed to have a grip on her that she couldn't escape. Another young man was accustomed to using sex to escape unwanted emotions in his past. His sexual past affected his ability to deal with his emotions and inhibited him from opening his heart to his wife.

From unwanted memories to sexually transmitted diseases, sexual encounters can leave a lasting negative imprint on our lives. For those who have committed to reserving sexual intimacy for marriage, continue to guard your hearts and bodies, because your future marriage will reap the rewards as you enter it with one less burden, as well as with the anticipation of mutual sexual discovery.

But for those who are struggling with a sexual past, be encouraged; we serve a God of restoration and grace. The road to healing and restored relationships may be difficult, but it is possible to let go of the burdens of your past. Philippians 3:13 tells us to forget what is behind and look toward what's ahead. Rather than allowing your past to hinder you, you can learn from it, allowing it to propel you into wholeness, healing, and newfound hope.

See chapter 8 for more on dealing with your sexual past.

18. I know going all the way can be damaging to a relationship, but how far is too far?

I'm always approached by young men and women who believe in reserving sex for marriage but want to know what they can do physically in the meantime.

This is a hard question to answer, because I don't view sex as a specific act; rather, I see it as a spectrum of experiences culminating in sexual intercourse. If sex is a spectrum of experiences, then where does a person draw the line? And if one experience leads to the next, should this spectrum even be breached?

It's important to be aware of the different stages of intimacy.

Behavioral scientist Desmond Morris states that there are twelve stages of marital intimacy, ranging from eye contact to sexual intercourse. While these stages are all part of the sexual experience, many are not sexual in and of themselves. To help determine proper physical boundaries, I've grouped these twelve stages into three categories of interaction:

Physical Interaction: The Green Zone. No matter where you go, it's easy to see that physical interaction between human beings is part of everyday life. From a handshake at the office to a hug at lunch between friends, physical touch is part of expressing love and gratitude to the people in our lives. The first category of interaction can be seen as just that, acts of physical communication. These acts may or may not be expressions of sexual affection:

- Eye to body
- Eye to eye
- Voice to voice
- Hand to hand
- Hand to shoulder
- Hand to waist

Affectionate Interaction: The Yellow Zone. Acts in the second category of interaction carry a lot more weight because of their exclusivity. These acts are reserved for the expression of affection between two people. Though these actions may be safely used in a healthy relationship to display affection when there is a clear understanding of limits and values between both people, they should always be used with caution because they can transform into expressions of sexual desire. They should be used to communicate love rather than to create lust.

- Mouth to mouth
- Hand to head
- Hand to body (not including breast or below the waist)

Sexual Interaction: The Red Zone. No matter how you perceive it, interactions in the third category are always sexual. They elicit a sexual desire based on a biological response. God wired our bodies this way, and these acts display a clear intent to engage in sexual interaction. These acts should be reserved entirely for married couples; all others will find themselves entering a danger zone, a place of vulnerability without permanent stability.

• Mouth to breast
• Hand to genitals
• Sexual intercourse

When it comes to assessing "how far is too far," it's important to remember that above and beyond keeping physical boundaries, our motives, thoughts, and beliefs ultimately determine whether our actions honor self, others, and God.

As Christians, we are called to do what's best and not just what is okay. Rather than fixating on how far we can go physically, we should align our actions with how holy we can be in our interactions with the opposite sex. Instead of looking at sexual purity as a list of do's and don'ts, we should see it as the means to protect our hearts, guard our minds, and preserve our bodies for the experience of true love.

19. I am dating a Christian, but our spirituality never seems to come up. What do I do?

One thing I love about my husband is that I always know I am a topic of conversation throughout his day. It's true. I run into his coworkers and friends all the time, and they always seem to know exactly what is going on in my life (even my hair appointments). They tell me that he's always talking about me and that we seem to be so in love. Well, they're right. We are so in love.

When you love something or someone, you will find that love overflowing from your lips whether you want it to or not. John talks about me all the time because I am on his mind and in his heart. I am a huge part of his life. He can't separate his existence from mine, and I feel the same way about him.

Music, sports, movies, books. Career, future, goals, dreams. Discussing these things is an important part of getting to know the person before you. But if these things continuously trump spiritual conversation in your life, then it's time to get real with where your heart or your partner's heart is really focused.

Luke 6:45 puts it this way: "The mouth speaks what the heart is full of." You will get to know your partner's heart by hearing what comes out of their mouth. The things they talk about reveal their passions and loves. If their heart is truly filled with love for God, it will be spewing from their mouth in routine conversation. You won't have to search hard for it if it's there.

But what if it's not? If your relationship does not reflect the faith and commitment to God that you would like it to, then it's time to do something about it. Be an active participant in your relationship by bringing up the things that are important to you. You are responsible for yourself, so take ownership of your relationship as well.

Give your partner the benefit of the doubt, and lead the way by sharing your heart about your relationship with God, and then wait to see what happens. In some cases, your partner may need encouragement to go in the right direction, time to build trust, or a deeper level of commitment before opening up about such important things. But in most cases, silence indicates something is not quite right.

Whether it's you or your partner who seems to be the "undercover Christian," ask yourself why.

If you identify with the life of a silent Christian, it's time to search your heart. What is the status of your commitment to God, and how much time, energy, and communication are you devoting to that relationship? You would do well to make sure your relationship with God is in order before you continue in a relationship with another.

On the other hand, if you find yourself in a relationship in which your partner is not responding to or connecting with your spirituality, it's time to face the reality of *their* spiritual journey by asking questions and having an important conversation about where that person stands. More than likely, you already know.

My friend Lisa finally came to terms with this possibility and began asking her boyfriend questions about his relationship with God. They were questions that she had been waiting for him to answer through his life and conversation, but all she was getting was silence. When she finally asked him about it, she realized she had to let go of the hope she had been hanging onto. She learned that her boyfriend had grown up in church but did not identify with the concept of being in relationship with God. He was unable to connect with her in this way and did not seem to understand why this difference in their lives was such a big deal. Lisa finally acknowledged that her attraction to her boyfriend was based on what she hoped he would be, rather than on who he was.

Relationships are pretty simple: what you see is what you get. What you see in your dating relationship likely is the *best* that person has to offer. It's problematic when we live for what we hope for in a relationship rather than for what the relationship actually is. If you can't see it, hear it, or feel it, then it probably isn't there.

Get to the bottom of who you are and where you are on your spiritual journey, and then do the same with the person standing before you. There is so much joy to be gained when you are in the right relationship. Don't waste your time living in a dream with one partner, when you could be experiencing a healthy reality with another.

20. Is it okay for a Christian to date a non-Christian?

Let's start off by breaking down the meaning of *okay*. If by *okay* you are hoping that entering into a relationship with a non-Christian will not condemn you to the depths of hell, then yes, it's okay. Simply put, dating a non-Christian is not a sin. The Bible discusses the hardships that come with being married to a nonbeliever, but it doesn't discuss the specifics of dating a non-Christian, because dating did not exist in biblical times.

But if by *okay* you mean a healthy, wise choice of a partner who might become your future mate, my answer is a loud and clear NO (capitalized for even more emphasis).

Two particular verses come to mind when people ask me this question. The first is 1 Corinthians 10:23. In a letter to a new group of believers, Paul explains what the church should partake in and what it should refrain from. They had so many questions about what was okay and what was not okay for them in their new lives as Christians. Paul answers them in a way that pushes their thinking to the next level. He challenges the church not to ask "Is it okay?" but to ask "Is it beneficial?" Will this benefit your life and your relationship with God, or will it cause you to remain the same (or even cause you to take a few steps back)? God is not calling you to go after what is acceptable in your life; he is calling you to do what is *best* for your life. It might be okay to date a non-Christian in that it's not a sin, it won't kill you, and it might feel pretty good. But you do yourself a grave injustice when you enter a relationship that is only okay, rather than what is best.

The second verse that has helped shape my beliefs on this topic is 2 Corinthians 6:14, which says, "Do not be yoked together with unbelievers. For what do righteousness and wickedness have in common? Or what fellowship can light have with darkness?" Other versions of the Bible read, "Don't team up with those who are unbelievers" (NLT), and "Do not be bound together with unbelievers" (NASB).

No matter how you view it, dating is a precursor to marriage, and marriage is definitely a "binding" experience. No two are joined as closely as a husband and a wife, a union that the Bible describes as "becoming one" (Gen. 2:24). It's the exciting, incredible, and excruciating process of taking two people with their own likes and dislikes, personality differences, and different backgrounds and molding them into one. And let me tell you, a lot of blood, sweat, and tears goes into this process. It's hard work!

God knows the difficulty involved in uniting two different people, and he encourages his children to choose someone with whom they can become fully one emotionally, physically, and spiritually.

This makes sense for two reasons. First, we are holistic beings. In order to really connect, we need to find a spouse with whom we can bind ourselves on every single level, mind, body, and soul. You can't be missing a component if you are to be fully united. But so many young Christians attempt to get into this process with someone they connect with emotionally and physically, but not spiritually. They settle for two out of three and assume that this is as good as it gets.

This way of thinking is sure to cause serious disappointment and broken hearts. It's one of the most devastating things in the world to be married to someone who doesn't share in every part of your life. I'm talking not only about Christians marrying non-Christians but even Christians marrying Christians who are not as committed to God as they are.

The second reason it makes sense to choose someone you can become fully one with on all levels is that, statistically, the most successful marriages consist of two people who are joined by a higher calling. For Christians, this higher calling is found in relationship with Jesus Christ. It's a calling that motivates you to love, to forgive, and to put aside self to glorify God through the relationship he has given you. It's a calling to represent Jesus to everyone around you, most specifically to your spouse.

Entering marriage puts you in the most vulnerable state of your life. Being married gives the person standing before you the ability to hurt you in a far deeper way than anyone else in this world can, and let me tell you, there are times when this happens. My husband and I have hurt each other out of selfishness and immaturity, and both of us will tell you that there are moments when forgiveness, love, and selflessness are the last things on our minds. This is when the beauty of our higher calling shines the brightest.

Because my husband has a relationship with Jesus, I can trust that this higher calling in his life will challenge and motivate him to love me, to forgive me, and to serve me, even when his hurt emotions are telling him not to. And it does. He loves me in a way that no human can possibly love on his own. Because it's not his own. God is at work in his life, producing fruit that I can fully trust, honor, and give myself to. Our relationship with God binds us together spiritually, but it also enables us to love each other unconditionally. I can't imagine giving myself to a man who is motivated by anything less than that divine calling.

So, yes, you can date a non-Christian if you want to risk pain, heartbreak, and grave disappointment. But you can also decide to be called into the privilege and honor and joy of dating someone who can connect with your spirit and your heart. You are entitled to find a true soul mate, a partner who can identify with the deepest parts of who you are.

But the choice is yours to make.

21. What about "missionary dating"?

I recently spoke with a young man who was involved in a dating relationship with a troubled young woman. Her life had been filled with pain, and she was dealing with the devastating shame that resulted from poor decisions she had made. She was looking for unconditional love, for someone to rescue her from the pain of her past and free her from the struggles of her present.

In walks Mr. Prince Charming. He had been born and raised in church, and his relationship with God was foundational to his life. He wanted to share God's love with the world, and especially with this five-foot-four bombshell who was looking for love. He was determined to show her Jesus' love no matter the cost. Just as he had been rescued from his sin, he wanted to rescue her, free her from her shame, and show her that she was worth being loved, forgiven, and accepted.

And so began their roller-coaster dating relationship. She continuously hurt him out of the overflow of the dysfunction and pain in her life; he continuously forgave her, letting her hurt him again and again and again.

When I questioned him regarding this unhealthy relationship, he responded sincerely by asking, "Isn't this what Jesus would do?"

The answer to that question is an enthusiastic, "Absolutely!" This is just what Jesus would do, and this is what Jesus did and continues to do for countless broken men and women. He takes them in, cleanses their sin, forgives their past, and replaces their shame with love, acceptance, and honor.

Jesus does this so well. Why, then, do we feel the need to take his place?

There is a huge difference between loving like Jesus loves and actually taking Jesus' place in someone's life. This, I'm afraid, is what happens in "missionary dating" — dating a nonbeliever in the hope of leading them to Jesus.

Well-meaning people who want to love someone into the kingdom of God end up taking on the role of God in their significant other's life. No matter who you are or how wonderful you may be, humans tend to be dreadfully awful stand-ins for almighty God. We can't fill that role because we were never meant to.

Missionary dating does more harm than good. In trying to bring someone into the kingdom, missionary daters can end up standing in the way of healing, repentance, and a relationship with the Lord. And oftentimes, instead of drawing their significant other into the light and love of Jesus, they find themselves slowly sinking into the darkness of poor decisions, sinful behavior, and subtle compromises.

If you know someone who is broken or hurting, love that person by leading them to the right source for help. Rather than taking their issues upon your shoulders, guide them to a youth leader, counselor, pastor, or trusted mentor, someone who can help them through the process of healing without becoming an obstacle or developing an emotional attachment.

Seek to show the love of Christ to the world around you without the complications of romantic feelings so you can love and serve freely and selflessly.

And when you enter a romantic relationship, do it with someone who can reflect Jesus' love back to you.

22. How do I deal with insecurities in a relationship?

Many of our insecurities stem from wrong beliefs about who we are. From the time we are children, wrong beliefs can be placed on us by parents, friends, family, sinfulness, and even ourselves. These beliefs shape our view of self and, in turn, how we act and how we react to the world around us. They are like lenses through which we take in reality; if our lenses are dirty, everything we see is blemished as well. When you live with insecurities, you interpret everything negatively, including your relationships.

I knew someone who had a really hard time with this. She struggled with insecurities and negative thoughts and feelings about herself — from her weight to her looks to her personality deficits and character flaws. She magnified these weaknesses and began to believe that other people saw her the same way. Her insecurities crept into her relationship with her husband. Though he was only trying to encourage her and help her to grow, she interpreted all of his actions as highlighting her weaknesses. Her negativity wore on their relationship, forming a barrier of mistrust and doubt between them.

It's important not to minimize insecurities. A person cannot just wish negative thoughts and feelings away. Years of negative buildup may require years to remove, but with God's help and lots of effort, miracles really can happen, even in a person's emotional world.

It takes lots of reflection and hard work to identify negative thoughts and beliefs and then replace them with God's truth, to see yourself from God's perspective. Some people's insecurities run so deep that they need the help of a professional counselor. Others may consider the following steps to get them on their way:

1. *Keep a journal to track your thinking.* Insecurity can always be traced to a pattern of negative thinking. You have to identify the problematic thinking in order to change it. Consider recording in a journal the negative beliefs and statements you find yourself thinking throughout the day. (Examples: "No one could ever love me." "I'm ugly." "I have nothing to offer.") Then counter each of these statements with God's truth. (See chap. 3 for a list.) Begin to recognize your negative thinking so that you can start replacing it with the truth.

2. *Surround yourself with people who will encourage you.* Your beliefs are shaped by the people you spend the most time with. You are the most influential voice in your life, but your closest friends and family are the second most influential voices. Surround yourself with healthy people who love and respect you enough to speak encouraging and

uplifting truths into your life, people who will keep you grounded and keep you on track, people who will reflect to you the value that you already possess. While others can't remove your insecurities, they can aid you in the process of developing healthy thinking.

In order to freely love and be loved, you must get to the root of your insecurities, allowing God to transform your heart and renew your thinking. It's time to uncover the truth about how valuable you really are.

23. Should you ever date someone you wouldn't consider marrying?

There seem to be two mindsets on the purpose of dating.

Some people see dating as a fun opportunity to get to know others. It's a time for trying new things, meeting new people, and partaking in new experiences. It's a chance to get to know yourself more as a result of your interactions with others, and the more interactions, the better.

For others, dating is a choice to enter a relationship with someone who has the potential to become a spouse. It's a time of discovery intended to end in marriage, so the less time wasted the better.

I think it's important to take both views into consideration. The best kind of dating is a combination of the two: it's a special time of getting to know yourself more and interacting with others, as well as the learning process through which you find a spouse.

No matter how many fun experiences you throw into the mix, dating is a lot of hard work. It involves conflict, communication, and compromise — three difficult exchanges. If you are going through the work of dating, why not have the reward of a lifelong partner in mind? Dating without intending to marry is akin to auditing four years of college — putting in all the time, energy, and hard work without attaining a degree.

Should you ever date someone you wouldn't marry? My personal answer is no. There is little to be gained from dating someone you would never marry that you couldn't glean from being friends with them. Instead of dating someone you would never marry, invest in healthy friendships and reap the same rewards without running additional risks.

24. How do I deal with the pain of a breakup?

I regularly receive email from people who are dealing with heartbreak. Heartbreak is devastating, regardless of who initiates the breakup. But there is always hope for healing. Here are some steps to get you on your way:

1. *Take time to be broken.* One way to keep a broken heart from healing is to try to get over it too quickly. Sometimes quick fixes end up covering wounds instead of healing them. It has been said that some people take half as much time to heal after a broken relationship as the time the relationship lasted. Though there is no scientific evidence for that rule, there is truth in saying that the greatest component of healing is time. Allow yourself time to grieve the loss of a relationship. As with any loss, a person grieving a breakup passes through five stages: denial, anger, bargaining, depression/sadness, and acceptance. Don't enter another relationship before you have worked through all of these stages.

2. *Take time to forgive.* A breakup can leave you feeling bitterness, anger, and rage. Even mutual breakups can leave you feeling insecure, wondering if you measure up. When faced with this mixture of unpleasant emotions, it's easy to play the blame game. It's easy to look at the hurts you have

endured, feel the injustice against you, and find yourself hoping for revenge. But no one is hurt by your inability to let go of the past more than yourself. Harboring unforgiveness is like drinking acid; it will destroy you from the inside out. It's important to recognize the pain you are holding on to so that you can begin to let it go, handing those feelings to the only One who can bring healing.

3. *Pursue growth.* If time is the first piece of the puzzle, then growth is the next. If you don't pursue growth, time alone will only dull the pain, not heal it. The season after a breakup should be more than just a time to wait around for the next relationship; it should be a time of self-discovery and awareness, transforming you into an even better version of yourself. It's a chance to let go of the past and focus on the present. It's an opportunity to learn from your mistakes and address your struggles, to work on your weaknesses and highlight your strengths. Don't let time pass in vain. Do things you've always wanted to do, go places you've always wanted to go, and become the person you've always dreamed of being. Allow each moment to stretch you toward awareness, growth, and maturity.

4. *Look for new opportunities.* The saying goes that as one door closes, another opens. The same goes with broken hearts. Saying no to one person leaves you available to say yes to another. I am so thankful for the many doors that God closed in my past, because they were doors I probably never would have closed on my own, and they are doors that would have led to further pain and deeper rejection down the line. Rather than allowing heartbreak to paralyze or confine you, you must see it as a chance to try again, trusting God with your every step. Even in your heartbreak, God has a purpose. Nothing says it quite like the Rascal

Flatts song "Bless the Broken Road," which my Texan friends played at their wedding. For each of them, their past heartbreaks were simply part of a "grander plan."

Even in your heartbreak, God has a plan. Take the time to heal, grow, and open your eyes to the next step. Who knows? True love might be just around the corner.

25. Does God have only one person in mind for me?

I have a love-hate relationship with this question. I love the idea that God has created one person specifically for you, but I hate the stress that comes with figuring out who that person is. It's like finding a needle in a haystack, or so it seems.

There's lots of disagreement on this question. In college, two incredible professors whom I adored passionately disagreed on it. Even my husband and I disagree. Yes, we ended up together, and we can't imagine ourselves being with anyone else, nor would we want to be with anyone else, but we still differ on this question.

So who's right?

It doesn't really matter.

That may not be the answer you were looking for, but it's legit! I believe this is one of those questions we are free to answer whatever way makes sense to us. Aside from the unique story of Adam and Eve, there really isn't much scriptural evidence to support the claim that God "creates" just one person for each of us.

Regardless of how you choose to answer this question, some things are certain when it comes to finding "the one."

1. *God grants us wisdom and discernment to make good relationship choices and gives us clear guidelines in his Word.* I believe that the bounty of Scripture passages discussing the characteristics of a good husband or a good wife places cer-

tain responsibilities on our shoulders (e.g., Prov. 31:10 – 31; 18:22; 14:1; 12:4; 1 Tim. 5:14; 1 Peter 3:1 – 6). God gives us some important information to guide us when it comes to finding and marrying "the one." Like it or not, you are not going to open your door one day to find the partner of your dreams standing there, waiting to be yours. Whether or not God has one person in mind for you, it's still your responsibility to make positive decisions to get yourself to that person. You must engage in the process of getting to know God, others, and especially yourself. It's vital to get to know God's Word, which tells you not only what to look for but also what you should strive to become.

2. *We are free to choose whom we will marry, and ultimately we will reap what we sow, so we must choose wisely.* In some countries, a person has limited freedom to choose a mate. (My grandma was from one of these countries, but even so, she engaged in a healthy, lifelong, and love-filled marriage.) But most of us will stand at the end of the aisle with the person of our choosing, probably with little or no objection from the people in our lives. It's simply our choice. Whether or not God has one person in mind for you, it's up to you to identify and choose that person. Anyone who is aligned with God's Spirit has a huge advantage in this process. He will guide and lead you, prompting your heart and mind along the way. It's important to trust God in this process, but I believe that God is also trusting *you* — trusting you to read his Word, seek good counsel, and get yourself in a healthy place so that your marriage will be healthy as well.

3. *When you say "I do," you enter a sacred union with another. That person automatically becomes the one you choose for the rest of your life.* It's best not to get hung up on whether you

married "the one," because it really doesn't matter once you are married. That pressure can do more harm than good. Once you have dated inward, outward, and upward, have assessed a healthy, loving relationship, and have decided to enter marriage, the person standing before you becomes "the one." It may sound simple, but I say this from the perspective of counseling countless men and women who have walked into my office fifteen years or more into their marriages, wondering if they married the right person. Doubt, regret, and fear plague them, and the prospect of a divorce looms large because they worry that they have chosen the wrong mate. It's a lot of pressure to discern whether you've married "the one," but imagine the pressure of trying to fit the mold of being "the one." It's bound to lead to a letdown. If you have done everything in your power to become a healthy individual and to choose a healthy partner, then rest assured that you are entering a nourishing marriage. The moment you say "I do," you have found the one whom you will choose to love and commit to for the rest of your life. Thankfully, dating provides you with ample opportunity to consider any doubts and concerns about the relationship you are in and to walk away before you've sealed the deal.

Ultimately, it doesn't matter whether God has only one person in mind for you, because either way the result is the same. There will come a season in your life in which you have to make some serious decisions regarding dating and marriage. For those of you who believe that there is only one person out there for you, be encouraged by that, and then work to get yourself to a healthy place so that when that person comes along, you can recognize him or her in the crowd of potential partners you will come across. For those of you who think there are many valid options, the same goes for you. Invest in the process of becoming the best you can be so that you are able to wisely choose the person you will commit to for the rest of your life. Either way, when you say "I do," you are looking into the eyes of *your* one, "'til death do us part."

NOTES

1. Sharon Jason, "Look-Alikes, Not Just Opposites, Can Attract Too," *USA Today*, June 21, 2012, *http://usatoday30.usatoday.com/news/health/wellness/story/2012-06-18/lookalikes-attract/55720994/1*, accessed April 2013.

2. Rober Alberti and Michael Emmons, *Your Perfect Right: Assertiveness and Equality in Your Life and Relationships* (Atascadero, CA: Impact Publishers, 1970), 38.

3. Mayo Clinic Staff, "Reactive Attachment Disorder," July 6, 2011, *http://www.mayoclinic.com/health/reactive-attachment-disorder/DS00988*, accessed March 2013.

4. P. Roger Hillerstrom, *Intimate Deception: Escaping the Trap of Sexual Impurity* (Sisters, OR: Multnomah, 1988), 37.

5. 1 Thess. 4:3 – 5; Heb. 13:4; Eph. 5:3; 1 Cor. 6:18; just to name a few passages.

6. Hillerstrom, *Intimate Deception*, back cover.

7. Mark Gungor, "The Damage of Sexual Promiscuity," *Laugh Your Way to a Better Marriage*, March 16, 2009, *http://www.laughyourway.com/blog/the-damage-of-sexual-promiscuity/*, accessed March 2013.

8. Rob Bell, *Sex God: Exploring the Endless Connections between Sexuality and Spirituality* (Grand Rapids, MI: Zondervan, 2007).

9. There is always the potential for forgiveness and restoration in a marriage if both parties are willing, though many theologians agree that Scripture clearly gives two grounds for divorce: (1) sexual immorality or adultery (Matt. 5:32) and (2) abandonment by an unbeliever (1 Cor. 7:15). Many pastors and counselors add abuse and addictions as reasonable grounds for divorce.

ABOUT THE AUTHOR

Before anything else in her life, Debra Fileta is a woman passionately in love with her Lord. That love has been the driving motivator propelling her forward in her pursuits as a wife, a mother, a licensed professional counselor, and an author.

Debra is married to the true love of her life, a wonderful man who pushes her to pursue her dreams and is essentially her "living laboratory of love." She considers every day to be an experiment in the pursuit of true love. She and John are parents to bright Ella and joyful Elijah. They currently reside in Hershey, Pennsylvania. (And yes, it really does smell like chocolate!)

Debra is a Licensed Professional Counselor specializing in dating, marriage, and relationship issues. She works in private practice with both individuals and couples. Prior to her private practice, she worked in a spectrum of mental health settings, including adolescent residential facility, inpatient psychiatric care, and the public school system.

Debra experienced an enrichment of her own life and relationships resulting from her professional education and practice, and her passion is sharing that information with young adults. For relationship articles, dating advice, or to contact Debra, be sure to visit her website (*www.truelovedates.com*) and follow her on Twitter (@ DebFileta).

Share Your Thoughts

With the Author: Your comments will be forwarded to the author when you send them to *zauthor@zondervan.com*.

With Zondervan: Submit your review of this book by writing to *zreview@zondervan.com*.

Free Online Resources at

www.zondervan.com

Daily Bible Verses and Devotions: Enrich your life with daily Bible verses or devotions that help you start every morning focused on God. Visit www.zondervan.com/newsletters.

Free Email Publications: Sign up for newsletters on Christian living, academic resources, church ministry, fiction, children's resources, and more. Visit www.zondervan.com/newsletters.

Zondervan Bible Search: Find and compare Bible passages in a variety of translations at www.zondervanbiblesearch.com.

Other Benefits: Register to receive online benefits like coupons and special offers, or to participate in research.